# 1 Wee

## SPOTLIGHT ON

# SPECIAL EDUCATIONAL NEEDS: ✓

# SPECIFIC LEARNING DIFFICULTIES

IU

## DOROTHY SMITH

A NASEN Publication

Published in 1996

© Dorothy Smith

All rights reserved. No part of this publication may be reproduced or transmitted in any form or by any means, electronic, mechanical, photocopying, recording, or otherwise without the prior permission of the publishers, except for Appendix 1 on pages 76–78.

ISBN 0 906730 89 9

The right of Dorothy Smith to be identified as author of this work has been asserted by her in accordance with the Copyright, Designs and Patents Act 1988.

Published by NASEN Enterprises Ltd.
NASEN Enterprises is a company limited by guarantee, registered in England and Wales. Company No. 2637438.

Further copies of this book and details of NASEN's many other publications may be obtained from the Publications Department at its registered office: NASEN House, 4/5, Amber Business Village, Amber Close, Amington, Tamworth, Staffs. B77 4RP.
Tel: 01827 311500; Fax: 01827 313005

Copy editing by Nicola von Schreiber.
Cover design by Graphic Images.
Typeset in Times by J. C. Typesetting and printed in the United Kingdom by Stowes, Stoke-on-Trent.

# SPOTLIGHT ON SPECIAL EDUCATIONAL NEEDS: SPECIFIC LEARNING DIFFICULTIES

# Contents

# Acknowledgements

The author and publishers wish to express their grateful thanks to Alec Williams and Mike Hinson for their helpful suggestions and comments.

The extract from the *Individual Reading Analysis* © by Denis Vincent and Michael de la Mare, 1989, 1992 on page 37; the extract from the *New Reading Analysis* © by Denis Vincent and Michael de la Mare, 1985 on page 38; the extract from the *Graded Word Reading List* © NFER-NELSON 1992 on page 40 are all reproduced with the permission of the publishers NFER-NELSON, Darville House, 2 Oxford Road East, Windsor SL4 1DF.

Please note that all children's names in the examples quoted have been changed to preserve their anonymity.

# SPOTLIGHT ON SPECIAL EDUCATIONAL NEEDS: SPECIFIC LEARNING DIFFICULTIES

## Introduction

*Some children may have significant difficulties in reading, writing, spelling or manipulating number, which are not typical of their general level of performance. They may gain some skills in some subjects quickly and demonstrate a high level of ability orally, yet may encounter sustained difficulty in gaining literacy or numeracy skills. Such children can become severely frustrated and may also have emotional and/or behavioural difficulties.*

*(Code of Practice*, para. 3:60)

Specific learning difficulties is one of the eight categories of special educational needs which has its own separate section within the *Code of Practice* (DfEE, 1994). This document adds in brackets 'for example dyslexia' to its section on specific learning difficulties within the chapter on criteria for statutory assessment (*Code of Practice*: Chapter 3). The main thrust of this publication will be specific learning difficulties in its widest sense. However, it should be noted that this term is now often used synonymously with dyslexia by writers on the subject.

### History

This distinction between a general learning difficulty and a specific learning difficulty has taken many years to be generated. Although it was recognised by some educators that there were individuals whose attainments in reading did not appear to match their probable intellectual levels and whose literacy problems were difficult to help, there were others who dismissed these suppositions. In fact the phrase 'word-blind' was coined as far back as 1896 and from this the dyslexia movement was born. However, official educational recognition of what now is termed 'specific learning difficulties' only appeared with the publication of the *Warnock Report* in 1978 (although dyslexia was recognised under the *Chronically Sick and Disabled Persons Act* of 1970).

Thus within the past hundred years much has been achieved by individuals and organisations in order to gain recognition for adults and young people who have been assigned as 'dyslexic' or who now have been given the label as having 'specific learning difficulties'. Over the years the emphasis on the problem being solely one of reading difficulties has changed to encapsulate other factors, in particular the written word via spelling problems.

## Definition

One of the resulting difficulties was that of an acceptable definition. Changes occurred as educators tried to bring into a short statement the many problems that may be discovered in an individual with such difficulties. For example:

Children with specific learning difficulties are those who, in the absence of sensory defect or overt organic damage, have an intractable learning problem in one or more of reading, writing, spelling and mathematics, and who do not respond to normal teaching.

(Tansley and Panckhurst, 1981)

The above definition does not fully explain the underlying problems and features of those specific difficulties that are deeply established in certain individuals. Up to 10 per cent of children have some specific problems and about 4 per cent will be severely affected according to the British Dyslexia Association (*The Dyslexia Handbook,* 1995). The following interpretation may be more acceptable as it includes some of the other factors that may be present. This version is a compilation from varying sources.

Specific learning difficulties are significant problems of:
• synthesising (bringing together information within the brain);
• organising (making sense and order of this information);
• memorising (holding onto this information in order to use it at will).

These severe problems which restrict the individual's proficiencies in information processing produce an intractable (or hard to shift) learning problem in some or all of the skills of:
• reading;
• spelling;
• written work;
• numeracy;
which does not respond to normal classroom teaching. If unrecognised there may be instances of secondary emotional/behavioural problems.

Invariably it is the individual's *working memory*, both visual and auditory (although for some, the problem may rest with only one of these), that is the key problem. The working memory is that part of the memory function which has to hold on to input collected from the senses (either immediate or brought back from long-term memory). This input or information has to be understood and organised (usually in some kind of sequence) before

6

being applied and acted upon in some form and then returned to the long-term memory store. Therefore, if the working memory is weak then any process which demands its use (such as reading, spelling, numeracy, self-organisation) will be impaired.

Pupils with specific learning difficulties can come from any socio-cultural background and their intelligence can be measured at any level. This makes it a slight problem for some parents and educators to understand the distinction between a general and a specific difficulty. What has to be remembered is that a general learning difficulty is where a pupil finds learning and acquiring skills a problem in every area of the curriculum. This special educational need is dealt with fully in *Learning Difficulties* by Sally Beveridge (one of the books in NASEN's *Spotlight on Special Educational Needs* series).

It is also important to remember that if a child has a problem which is *easily* dealt with and if it is one that *can* be helped within the resources of normal classroom teaching then by definition it cannot be severe or significant. However, as with all problems there is a continuum of need and teachers need to be aware of all aspects of specific learning difficulties, from mild to moderate to severe.

It is not the intention of this book to discuss why specific learning difficulties occur, either genetically or neurologically. The References and Further Reading section will guide the reader towards such publications. It is also not the intention to discuss the sub-sets of specific learning difficulties as indicated in the *Code of Practice* which could include areas such as dyslexia, dyspraxia, dyscalculia, dysgraphia and dysphasia. (Reference is made to these in the appendices as is scotopic sensitivity syndrome and ADD, attention deficit disorder.)

This book is intended to be a practical handbook based on the *Code of Practice*'s sections 3.60–3.63. The statements contained within these sections will be amplified, and practical advice and help for class and subject teachers and parents will be given.

The choice of a correct label can be important for the child. Some cope well with the term 'dyslexia' but others hate the thought of appearing different from their peers. The term 'learning different' is becoming accepted as an educational term and this can be explained to the child in a positive manner. The child is not lazy or unintelligent and there are areas in which he or she can cope in the same way as everyone else but also there are areas of difficulty, areas of difference. To help these latter areas means hard work but there are always ways to ease the problems or to find strategies of coping with them. Any label needs to be associated with explanations and these should be given in as positive a manner as possible.

7

# Identification

A great deal of work has gone into identifying what factors make up the profile of an individual with specific learning difficulties and researchers and other educators have identified various problems which can be present. It is accepted that there is a continuum of problems where specific learning difficulties are concerned. These problems range from those that are mild to those that are severe. Also, as individuals are not identical, their own particular problems need not be exactly similar to those of others. Because of the varied nature of specific learning difficulties and the way that young people learn their basic skills, some children's problems do not become apparent until the end of the primary or beginning of their secondary years. For some individuals specific learning difficulties are not suspected until examination work is started during further education. However, there are also those children who are thought to have specific learning difficulties before they start their school life.

It must be remembered whenever a child's performance is matched against any list of criteria which may indicate a specific problem that one must not leap to conclusions. Checklists or performance indicators only form part of the identification process. Also, in most cases there would have to be a cluster of problems which would be the trigger for later more detailed assessment. Observations of children's learning behaviours in both the class and the home often can alert parents and teachers to a problem in learning. These then can be explored in more detail and can be given attention. As will be stated later, it is also important to determine what the child *can* do as well as examining the areas of difficulty.

### Early Identification

The Code of Practice states:

> Because early identification should lead to a more timely assessment and intervention which in turn should avoid the escalation of a difficulty into a significant special educational need, it is important that any concern about a child's development and progress should be shared at the earliest possible moment.
>
> (*Code of Practice*, para. 5:16)

There are certain checklists provided for parents and professionals who work with pre-school and early years children which give indicators that could point to later specific learning difficulty problems (see the section on positive criteria in this chapter). What has to be remembered is that however helpful these indicators can seem, they are made up from some of the factors which can be found in the general course of learning in most children. Teachers have to be aware of when an apparent weakness might be developmental and routine and when it might cause concern. What appears to be far more important is to make sure that *all* pre-school children in nurseries and playgroups, and early years children in their reception school classes develop the mastery of certain 'early learning' skills if they are going to be able to learn to read and write successfully and to cope with later school life.

These areas are :

- visual perception (what the pupil actually sees on the page and elsewhere), visual discrimination (how the pupil is able to see differences between words, letters and numbers), visual sequencing (the ability to perceive letters and words in the correct order), visual categorisation (knowledge of visual similarities between words and letters) and visual memory;

- auditory perception (the pupil's ability to hear sounds), auditory discrimination (how the pupil is able to hear differences between sounds), auditory sequencing (the ability to hear letters and words in the correct order), auditory categorisation (knowledge of similarities between the sounds of words and letters) and auditory memory;

- visual motor processing (the ability to produce, usually in writing, what is seen) and fine motor control;

- early number concepts;

- early phonological awareness (eg rhymes and alliteration);

- expressive and receptive language knowledge and usage adequate for early learning;

- ability to understand, process (internalise and make sense of) and carry out spoken instructions;

- ability to organise and process (internalise and make sense of) thoughts in order to express needs.

9

If a child finds problems with any of these broad indicators then early teaching programmes can be set up because these skills form the basis of later more 'formal' learning. There are references to books in the References and Further Reading which give more detailed information about acquiring these necessary skills. Young children can be more easily identified as having potential learning problems if they show an uneven developmental profile where there are particular strengths and particular weaknesses.

It is possible to encounter problems when very early identification practices are set up. It may be that this 'labelling' could lead to lower or negative expectations being set in motion by those who come in contact with the young child. Also incorrect labelling may occur because the child might just be slower in developing the relevant skills. However, it is generally felt that early identification, if handled correctly and sensitively, can be more beneficial than disadvantageous. More precise identification can lead to better targeted teaching because of the detailed description gained of the pupil's strengths and weaknesses.

**Identification in the Primary Sector: Early Stages**

As has already been mentioned there are checklists which purport to determine if a child has a specific or dyslexic learning difficulty and these can be damaging if used indiscriminately and without care. Some of the indicators are found in children's general learning and, therefore, teachers should be concerned only if problems persist for longer than is realistically expected. However, such lists could be used as a starting point especially if several of the points are found within the child's development. Put into broad categories the following could be used:

*Language areas*

- history of delayed speech and language development;

- difficulty with pronouncing multi-syllabic words;

- difficulty with sequencing and ordering in speech and language;

- difficulty in word labelling retrieval (being able to remember a particular word in speech).

*Visual problems*
Discrimination and sequencing

• letter order confusion when reading;

• poor left–right discrimination;

• leaves letters out of words – puts letters in the wrong order;

• confusion of similar-looking letters;

• reversals of letters and figures;

• use of mirror writing.

Memory

• strange spelling patterns;

• difficulty in telling left from right;

• misreads core vocabulary.

*Auditory problems*
Discrimination and sequencing

• difficulty with sound blending;

• difficulty with phonological awareness (rhyming words, alliteration) and syllable beating and segmentation (understanding how words are divided into syllables or parts);

• confusion of similar-sounding letters.

Memory

• difficulty in remembering the order of the days of the week, months of the year, the alphabet.

*General*

- early clumsiness;

- poor concentration span;

- similar familial history;

- lacks self-confidence;

- has 'good' and 'bad' days.

---

*An example of how to use the above indicators to make an initial identification*

Jake is 6 years old and because of his good understanding of language and oral ability and because he can cope with all areas of the National Curriculum except for reading and recording his class teacher and parents queried specific learning difficulties. The following indicators were noted with information being given by his parents and his teacher.

*Language areas*

| | |
|---|---|
| - history of delayed speech and language development | no evidence |
| - difficulty with pronouncing multi-syllabic words | no problems |
| - difficulty with sequencing and ordering in speech and language | no problems |
| - difficulty in word labelling retrieval | no problems |
| *Visual problems*<br>*Discrimination and sequencing* | |
| - letter order confusion when reading | some evidence of problems ('on/now') |

| | |
|---|---|
| • poor left–right discrimination | some evidence of problems |
| • leaves letters out of words – puts letters in the wrong order | problems with copying |
| • confusion of similar-looking letters | problems with matching and recognising letters printed in different fonts |
| • reversals of letters and figures | 'b/d' confusion and some letters incorrectly oriented |
| • use of mirror writing | not seen |
| *Memory* | |
| • strange spelling patterns | as yet cannot spell |
| • difficulty in telling left from right | yes |
| • misreads core vocabulary | some problems seen |
| *Auditory problems*<br>*Discrimination and sequencing* | |
| • difficulty with sound blending | could not cope from whispered sounds/did not understand concepts of sameness and difference |
| • difficulty with phonological awareness (rhyming words, alliteration) and syllable beating and segmentation | understands the concept of rhyme and can syllable beat – can 'hear' and produce first sounds but not end sounds, seems to understand the concept of alliteration and has begun to read words with units of sounds, knows many letter sounds for saying and writing |

| | |
|---|---|
| • confusion of similar-sounding letters | 'd/t' confusion and 'e/i' when writing |
| **Memory** | |
| • difficulty in remembering the order of the days of the week, months of the year, the alphabet | problems here and has to use letter names as a prop when spelling |
| **General** | |
| • early clumsiness | no |
| • poor concentration span | yes |
| • similar familial history | father had spelling problems as a boy |
| • lacks self-confidence | where reading is concerned |
| • has 'good' and 'bad' days | no |

There are some indications that Jake may have some specific learning difficulties and so his progress will be closely monitored. Particular emphasis will be given to visual discrimination activities, oral work on sounds and games for core word learning. Shared reading will be carried out because of his antagonism for this activity and his parents will be given games to reinforce the in-school teaching. His parents were pleased that Jake's early language skills caused no problems.

**Identification in the Primary Sector: Later Stages**

As a child grows older and is seen to be failing at the basic skills of reading and spelling although coping orally and in the more practical areas, it is rather more easy to observe those 'performance indicators' which could indicate the specificity of the problem. These can be observed when the child is responding to classroom activities and are where:

- performance in literacy skills is at a lower level than could be expected from performance in other curriculum areas;

- performance is often inconsistent varying from day to day;

- performance is varied dependent upon the child's mood (however, it should be noted that this is not expressly a specific problem);

- oral language is often at a higher level than written language;

- reading is slow and lacking in fluency;

- there are problems with phonic decoding and synthesis when reading;

- there are problems with remembering core keywords both in reading and spelling;

- memory problems show themselves both with factual retention and more global recall;

- spelling is bizarre and, therefore, uncommunicable;

- words attempted for spelling contain incorrect letters and letter combinations for particular sounds;

- spelling is inconsistent with previously learnt words spelt both correctly and incorrectly in one piece of writing;

- there are problems with pronouncing multi-syllabic words;

- emotional/behavioural problems become evident because of lack of self-confidence and low self-esteem;

- there might be additional difficulties with speech, motor skills, directional and spatial awareness and numeracy and also there could be visual anomalies (see the problems with visual discrimination etc mentioned as factors in earlier years).

*An example of how to use the above indicators in later identification*
Lenny is 8 years 6 months and has been assessed by an independent educational psychologist who measured his IQ as 'high average'. His Key Stage 1 SATs results were 2s and 3s except for writing and spelling which were 1. The following indicators can be noted:

| | |
|---|---|
| • performance in literacy skills is at a lower level than could be expected from performance in other curriculum areas | yes and shows that he has good long-term global information for facts |
| • performance is often inconsistent varying from day to day | yes, he gets very tired |
| • performance is varied dependent upon the child's mood | does not appear so |
| • oral language is often at a higher level than written language | definitely |
| • reading is slow and lacking in fluency | is underachieving here and when he tries decoding this breaks fluency but he uses contextual clueing |
| • there are problems with phonic decoding and synthesis when reading | inefficient decoding skills (poor rhyming skills) |
| • there are problems with remembering core keywords both in reading and spelling | is acquiring a small sight word store for both reading and spelling |
| • memory problems show themselves both with factual retention and more global recall | poor short-term auditory memory but efficient long-term recall, has a better visual–verbal memory |

| | |
|---|---|
| • spelling is bizarre | some words |
| • words attempted for spelling contain incorrect letters and letter combinations for particular sounds | has started to use simple sounds for spelling but has problems with sequencing and directional confusion |
| • spelling is inconsistent with previously learnt words spelt both correctly and incorrectly in one piece of writing | yes |
| • there are problems with pronouncing multi-syllabic words | when younger |
| • emotional/behavioural behaviours become evident because of lack of self-confidence and low self-esteem | is poor at concentration and settling down to work |
| • there might be additional difficulties with speech, motor skills, directional and spatial awareness, and numeracy, and also there could be visual anomalies | no speech problems but handwriting is very weak and there is much evidence of visual directional confusion |

Because Lenny coped with reading at Key Stage 1 his problems did not become evident until later. His progress will be carefully monitored and particular attention will be given to building up his better sight memory store for reading and spelling and helping him to become more fluent by using his contextual ability with first letter(s) clues. Direct teaching will be given to 'rationalise' his phonic decoding and encoding skills going back to short vowels with onset and rime activities and building up from that. His parents will be encouraged to play rhyming games and share read.

## Identification in the Secondary Sector

As teacher awareness and knowledge of specific learning difficulties grows, there should be fewer pupils entering secondary schools who have not been identified and helped during their primary school years. However, it should be recognised that the educational demands are different and more demanding, especially where examination courses are concerned, than those experienced in primary education. Thus some students who coped satisfactorily during these earlier school years might find their specific learning difficulties causing them particular problems in the secondary sector.

There are certain characteristics which can be given to secondary teachers in order to alert them to any possible specific learning problem. These are:

- problems with note taking either orally or from blackboards/OHPs;

- production of work takes a long time;

- problems with essay writing because of organisational difficulties (loses the thread of thought with points written in random order, difficulties in deciding what is relevant and what is irrelevant, cannot carry out a discussion or argument on paper);

- problems with written work for although it may show satisfactory content the spelling is particularly weak, the handwriting is poor, the work is presented untidily, words are simple and there is little or no sign of proofreading;

- discrepancies shown between course and examination work;

- discrepancies shown between oral work and written work;

- apparent problems with memory and personal organisational skills (especially time allocation);

- problems with recall of words (especially technical ones or those connected with the particular course);

- problems with reading (in particular with coping with large amounts) and reading avoidance;

- problems in producing work at the expected level although apparently able and/or talented in certain areas.

It is not expected that all the above would be seen but subject teachers should be alert to any presenting problems.

18

*An example of how to use the above indicators in secondary identification*

Ben is 11 years 4 months and although he had some minor literacy problems in the primary sector he entered his secondary school with adequate reading and writing skills. However, in the first few weeks his subject area teachers were concerned about his ability to access the curriculum.

| | |
|---|---|
| • problems with note taking either orally or from blackboards/OHPs | found this particularly difficult |
| • production of work takes a long time | very little work produced |
| • problems with essay writing because of organisational difficulties | yes |
| • problems with written work | spelling weak but readable but layout is untidy |
| • discrepancies shown between course and examination work | not as yet seen |
| • discrepancies shown between oral work and written work | he rarely answers orally |
| • apparent problems with memory and personal organisational skills | great problems here |
| • problems with recall of words | no real problems here |
| • problems with reading and reading avoidance | no problems here |
| • problems in producing work at the expected level although apparently able and/or talented in certain areas | homework never completed, avoidance techniques seen |

When the co-ordinator of special needs observed Ben closely she found that his whole problems stemmed from an extremely weak auditory memory and weak listening skills which made it very difficult for him to listen to information, hold it, process it and recall it.

His subject area teachers were asked to :

- give him instructions in small steps so that he completes one part of a task at a time

- provide written or pictorial *aide-mémoires* for reference

- get him to repeat the activity to help hold and process the information

- check his homework diary. (He has to write the information correctly, understand what he has to do, complete the task satisfactorily, bring back the work to school, give it in.)

## Other 'Criteria'

Definitions and identification of specific learning difficulties can also relate to the following terms: exclusion criteria, positive signs criteria and discrepancy criteria. These terms are often used to either confirm or reject identification of specific learning difficulties in the educational domain. Therefore, it is necessary to describe these but care and consideration have to be used when taking them into account because of all the problems that can arise.

### Exclusion criteria

There is the possibility that learning difficulties occur because of other factors. These other areas which need checking are the medical areas of vision, hearing, speech, language, motor development and general health. Behavioural problems should also be noted. It should be stated that there are those educationists who feel that a child should not be labelled as having a specific learning difficulty if there have been problems such as:

- sensory impairment – vision/hearing problems (early or continuing);

- motor problems;

- language problems (low receptive language skills – understanding);

- physical problems such as difficulties with fine motor skills;

- health problems especially if these result in much absence;

- pre-school and continuing behavioural problems;

- frequent changes of school, inappropriate teaching, lack of early schooling;

- emotional problems (poor self-image/lack of motivation);

- environmental circumstances (problems at home/parental pressure);

- English as a second language.

The above list forms the exclusionary criteria which states that other causes of the learning difficulty should be excluded before the specificity of the problem can be determined.

However, it should be said that it is not really helpful to discuss this debate in any detail because if children have a learning problem one needs to help them overcome it. It can be pointed out that if the literacy (and/or any other learning) difficulty rapidly improves when any of the above problems are resolved and a structured programme of work is given then the original learning problem was possibly not long-term and, therefore, had its root in the 'other' problem. Here the staged approach should be helpful (see Classroom Strategies in Stages 1–3) in order to see whether help and support needs to be given just for a short period of time or whether it is really long-term and intractable and, therefore, by definition 'specific'.

*Discrepancy criteria*

The *Code of Practice* seems to imply that there have to be extreme discrepancies between how the pupil performs on 'appropriately administered standardised tests of cognitive ability or oral comprehension' and how the pupil performs on 'appropriately administered standardised reading, spelling or mathematics tests'.

It can be a problematic road to follow if one tries to compare attainment with likely capabilities. It is sensible to treat and interpret all scores with care and to use diagnostic tools in depth. However, where statutory assessments requests are concerned it appears that LEAs will ask for the discrepancy model to be carried out and the results used alongside other areas which will be discussed later in this book and particularly in IEPs and Specific Learning Difficulties.

## *Core subjects of the National Curriculum*

When schools are required to provide evidence for the LEA when statutory assessment is requested they have to provide information about the child's attainment in the core subjects of the National Curriculum measured against each other to see if there are extreme discrepancies. In practice, this generally means that the overall level for English is low while that for mathematics and/or science would be average or higher than average. However, one should be aware that some pupils may gain a below average level in mathematics because of dyscalculia or if SATs levels are used there may have been problems with the reading side to the questions. (When SATs take place readers are permitted for mathematics and science. Teachers should do their best not to penalise pupils with specific learning difficulties by insisting that they complete these papers unaided.)

## *The core language subject (English/Welsh)*

Also connected with the National Curriculum the child's attainments within one core subject (in particular English/Welsh) have to be seen to be discrepant. In practice, this would mean that a child's level in Attainment Target 1 (speaking and listening, oral in Welsh) would be at an average or above average level whereas Attainment Targets 2 and 3 (reading and writing) would be below average. Because specific learning difficulties does not fit into convenient patterns, there may be some pupils who would have problems with expressive language as has been mentioned previously.

## *Intelligence*

Another area dealing with the discrepancy model concerns the pupil's intelligence or cognitive ability. A consensus must be reached among those who have taught the pupil and who have 'closely observed' him or her, supported by cognitive ability or oral comprehension tests, that his or her abilities are significantly above the attainments in National Curriculum assessments and tests and/or above whatever is scored in reading, spelling or mathematics tests. There is the possible danger of subjective assessments being made here with teachers and/or parents believing that the pupil is more intelligent than academic or literacy tests imply. This favours the articulate pupil who is well able to express him or herself. Often it is not until an educational psychologist administers either the WISC (Wechsler

Intelligence Scale) or BAS (British Abilities Scale) intelligence tests that a truer indication of the child's cognitive ability becomes apparent. However, different tests bring different results and reading tests assess different areas of literacy. This is discussed below in Assessment. The *Code* calls for tests to be 'appropriately administered'. LEAs may be expected to determine if this is occurring. Whether or not this will happen remains to be seen.

There are limitations to intelligence tests. The scores need not be fixed throughout the child's life, although in practice they tend to show similar results if retested over a period of time. If one considers an IQ score of 100 and a 10-year-old pupil, one could expect a reading and a spelling age of 10 years. If this IQ score was 120 then on this basis one could expect a reading and a spelling age of 12 years. If the discrepancy criteria are brought into play, a 10-year-old with an IQ of 120 and reading and spelling ages of 8 years could be said to have disparities between the two scores which to some people would be very worrying. If this child had reading and spelling ages of 10 years, at age-appropriate level, would similar concerns exist? There is still a discrepancy. The word 'significant' can cause problems as its meaning cannot be readily understood or determined. Psychologists have 'significant criteria' built into their tests so that they are able to work out how scores match each other. For the non-psychologist using other methods of assessment, it is more difficult to determine what can be deemed significant or what can be said is severe or what could be said would be within the normal expected range. Teachers may have to use their subjective judgements or wait for psychological help.

*Positive signs criteria*

This method of identification assumes that there is measurable or discernible evidence which determines the presence of specific learning difficulties. Checklists have been devised which give such indicators as have already been mentioned. Often these merely form a list asking, for example, for signs of directional confusion, inability to sequence and recite the days of the week or months of the year, showing signs of cross-laterality, difficulties with tying shoelaces or standing on one leg, problems with learning tables, and producing spelling which is bizarre. However, it is not helpful to use tick lists for identification purposes as many children who can access the curriculum areas well and who can read and spell adequately also could show themselves to be positively 'dyslexic' in some respect. Also, there are often no accepted numbers of positive indications built into these checklists which would confer what would deem one person to have specific learning difficulties and another to be within the accepted learning range.

*Learning difference*

Identification can present many problems to both parents and teachers. The *Code of Practice* for statutory assessment procedures provides a set of criteria based on the discrepancy model with some additional 'positive signs'. But when teachers and parents first identify possible specific learning difficulties this is not for a request for a statement but in order to provide information about the individual in order to help his or her learning. Often teachers can look back into the child's educational history for this information and then feel they can find reasons for the learning problem. In this way they use the exclusionary criteria. When a child begins to fail to learn and one wants to know the reason for this, it can also appear to be helpful to look to the so-called 'positive' signs and from these attach the label of 'specific learning difficulties'.

However, individuals have different styles of learning. They have their own strengths and weaknesses. These strengths and weaknesses may show up in global areas of learning or in very particular processes. Also, individuals face up to their own problems in very different ways. Some have positive self-esteem and are confident in their own learning while others feel themselves to be failures and their self-esteems are very low. Often their self-image matches how their parents feel about the learning problem and, thus, it is important for parents to be helped to come to terms with their child's specific learning difficulties (see Parents).

To identify and then assess pupils correctly in order to help them overcome their problems teachers need to know how these children are 'learning different' and then to use their positive strengths to advantage when setting up learning programmes. Identification may arise from any source but then the more detailed assessments have to be made in order to maximise efficient teaching and learning for individuals.

# Assessment

It is important to be able to back up what one feels one has identified with some type of assessment technique which can be carried out within the school or with the help of external specialists.

## Teacher Assessment

Class teachers can start by using the child performance indicators that were mentioned above in Identification. However, there are also criteria-referenced and standardised tests which can be used by the class teacher, the special educational needs co-ordinator (SENCO) and the advisory and learning support teachers. By using these means of assessment, more detailed records can be written about the pupil's strengths and weaknesses. A profile should be built up using these performance indicators, criteria-referenced assessments and/or standardised tests.

*Criteria-referenced assessments*

These assessments look at how the pupils perform at whatever they are asked to work on. They can be swift to use and most can be administered in the classroom rather than making an issue of extracting the child into a separate room. The teacher can diagnose where there are strengths and weaknesses within an area of skills and, therefore, will gain more insightful information in order to build up the pupil's profile. Check-sheets can be used for recording such information.

In order to learn how to read and spell effectively, the young child should be competent in particular areas. These are readily identifiable and there are criteria checks which can be easily made within the classroom situation:

- for the visual areas (visual perception, discrimination, sequencing, categorisation and memory):
  *check with matching, 'odd one out', pictures, story sequencing, putting objects into categories and Kim's Game;*

- for the auditory areas (auditory perception, discrimination, sequencing, categorisation and memory):
  *check with phonological awareness activities such as rhyming activities, segmentation of words, beating the syllables in multi-syllabic words, giving similarities and differences in words, understanding of whispered blending, alliteration, onset and rime activities, the understanding of analogies (how one word can be changed to another by altering one or more letters);*

- for fine motor control competencies (visual motor processing and handwriting):
  *check with threading beads, colouring, drawing shapes, drawing a line between two lines, copying a few letters of the alphabet, hand control and pencil grip;*

25

- for specialised word knowledge (positional words eg left/right/up/down, book words):
  *check orally;*

- for early number concepts:
  *check with saying numbers 1–5, 6–10, 0 (when presented randomly) and writing these when asked, one-to-one correspondence;*

- for adequate expressive and receptive language knowledge and usage:
  *check with oral work in class;*

- for the ability to understand, process and carry out spoken instructions:
  *check with following simple instructions.*

When looking at a child's performance in the literacy areas, depending on the age and attainment of the particular individual, the following skills and sub-skills can be checked:

- reading
  *check through miscue analysis (plus the sub-skills of phonics, key words, phonological awareness, auditory and visual discrimination and sequencing);*

- spelling
  *check through miscue analysis (plus high-frequency word knowledge, auditory and visual discrimination and sequencing);*

- writing
  *check from examples of independent writing (plus handwriting).*

*Reading*

Miscue analysis forms the basis of reading assessment. Teachers have to determine how the pupil tackles unknown words and from this will be able to ascertain if he or she is a visual or phonic reader, if he or she tries unknown words or just waits to be told and whether contextual cueing is evident. When the child reads a passage which is slightly too difficult, the substitutions for unknown words can be analysed as:

|  | **Graphically correct** | **Graphically incorrect** |
|---|---|---|
| **Contextually correct** | write the response under this column if the first letter(s) is the same as the original<br><br>plus<br><br>if the response fits the context of the sentence | write the response under this column if the first letter(s) is *not* the same as the original<br><br>plus<br><br>if the response fits the context of the sentence |
| **Contextually incorrect** | write the response under this column if the first letter(s) is the same as the original<br><br>plus<br><br>if the response does *not* fit the context of the sentence | write the response under this column if the first letter(s) is *not* the same as the original<br><br>plus<br><br>if the response does *not* fit the context of the sentence |

*Other criteria assessments for reading:*

Diagnostic assessment can be obtained from:

- knowledge of the 250 basic core keywords (McNally and Murray) as sight words;

- knowledge of which individual letter sounds are known (consonants and short vowels);

- knowledge of other letter sound combinations (such as consonant digraphs and consonant blends);

- blending ability (can the child blend from whispered heard sounds, can the child blend and synthesise three-letter regular words, cvc/consonant–vowel–consonant, and four/five letter regular words);

- phonological awareness (such as giving rhyming words to a stimulus word, beating out syllables in words, understanding alliteration, word–sound association or analogies, giving particular sounds from beginnings, middles and ends of words);

- being able to hold sounds in the working memory and to repeat and/or blend them;

- being able to see differences and similarities between patterns and/or words, to find smaller words in longer ones.

*An example of a miscue analysis*

Billy is 8 years 9 months and the miscue analysis is taken from one of his chosen reading books which was above his readability level.

|  | **Graphically correct** | **Graphically incorrect** |
|---|---|---|
| **Contextually correct** | over/on<br>spacesuit/spacecraft<br>milk/milky<br>Venice/Venus<br>metal/meteor<br>branch/balance | |
|  | use/using<br>first/fastest<br>spent/speed<br>object/oxygen | |
| **Contextually incorrect** | break/bacon<br>helent/helmet<br>distance/direct<br>stared/stray | injured/linger |

Apart from one non-word, Billy's substitutions are real words and all but one starts with the correct letter. The majority of his substitutions are contextually correct. He seems to have a tendency to rush into words without checking, so this can be worked on. He does not seem to be totally sure about using the correct first two letters so all the consonant blends and digraphs should be checked and some work given on these. He then should be helped to cope with two-syllable words.

*An example of a pupil who has phonological problems in reading and is totally a visual reader*

Kylie is 7 years 8 months and is felt to be of generally average ability. She manages to remember the words from the reading scheme books but faced with unknown words she has no strategies for reading them. It was found that she had problems with:

- understanding the concept of rhyme;

- providing rhyming words to given stimulus words;

- beating the correct number of syllables in words;

- blending two-letters as she wanted to add an 'er' to the end letter (eg 'aper' for 'ap');

- knowing all the initial consonant blends and short vowels;

- cvc (consonant–vowel–consonant) blending from whispered sounds (only slightly better with onset and rime);

- when given lists of similar-sounding words tending to perseverate by becoming muddled and jumping back to a previous list.

A very structured phonic programme was worked out for Kylie starting with oral work on sounds (games for the home etc) and then three-letter word reading in two chunks (onset and rime). All work would be multi-sensory involving the use of plastic letters with much reinforcement. Reading through visual memory strategies would be continued.

*An example of a pupil who has a very limited visual memory for core and high-interest words but who can cope with the phonic side to reading*

Dean is an 8-year-old highly verbal non-reader whose excellent vocabulary gets in the way of any effective reading as he wants to make core keywords more interesting (eg 'weird' for 'with'). He has many visual directional problems and knows that he has seen words before but he cannot recall the label. He knows very few of the first 100 keywords and finds reading scheme books very difficult. Because he is strong phonically he wants to sound out and blend every unknown word (sometimes this does not work as in 's-h-o-u-t-e-d' and sometimes he does so in a somewhat idiosyncratic way as in 'ch-h-ill/chill' and 'bl-l-ack/black').

To help Dean's self-esteem the phonic programme is to be emphasised so that he learns the consonant digraphs and blends and the more usual vowel digraphs. The *Fuzzbuzz* series of books will be given because of their phonic emphasis. However, in order to build up his core words he will be given these with pictograms so that there will be an added marker to help him.

*Spelling*

As with reading, a miscue analysis of written work can give far more information than just looking at words learnt for a spelling test. The tester is able to determine at which stage of spelling acquisition is the speller and whether the attempts show knowledge of serial probability (the letters that can be written together) in the English spelling system. One can also check for:

- knowledge of core sight words;

- the ability to produce letters for sounds (initial consonants and short vowels, then other regular sounds such as consonant digraphs and consonant blends);

- the ability to spell regular phonemic words;

- being able to discriminate between similar sounds and being able to word–sound associate;

- the ability to see that words are similar or dissimilar and to be able to find small words in longer ones.

*An example of an analysis of a pupil's independent written work in order to work out an appropriate spelling programme*

Simone is 10 years 2 months who reads well and copes with subject areas.

| Reasonable | | Unreasonable | | Bizarre attempts | | Auditory confusion Directional confusion | |
|---|---|---|---|---|---|---|---|
| poket | pocket | sidd | side | sed | scared | jrops | drops |
| gos | goes | kip | keep | pus ten | person | ofer | over |
| sum | some | don | down | masha | match | nufer | another |
| cud | could | lan | land | tus | touch | hafing | having |
| gardun | garden | wet } | went | wassed | washed | | |
| mor | more | wen } | | madr | ? | bont | don't |
| rokit | rocket | mus | much | sau | ? | | |
| pepall | people | goin | going | wast | ? | | |
| buy | bye | frst | first | sotid | ? | | |
| wen | when | calld | called | fiming | ? | | |
| flor | floor | hoosing | housing | | | | |
| cums | comes | flas | flash | | | | |
| | | riat | right | | | | |
| | | nir | near | | | | |
| | | sedi | said | | | | |
| 28% | | 36% | | 24% | | 12% | |

(reasonable = letter patterns found in the English spelling system
unreasonable = some visual or phonemic attempts seen
bizarre = cannot be read by the reader)

Simone has many problems in the acquisition of spelling and her written work does not always communicate because she has many problems with the sound–symbol system. Because of her difficulties with medial consonants, word endings and auditory confusion, she should be checked for any present or past hearing and speech problems. There are keywords incorrectly spelt so it is probably best to build up her common word knowledge by visual means before starting to build on her basic phonemic knowledge.

Apart from using pieces of independent written work for analysis there are passages for dictation that can be given. One set written for different spelling levels or chronological age levels has been compiled by Margaret Peters.

---

*An example of an analysis of a pupil's spelling using Peters' Diagnostic spelling assessment at the 9/10 years level*

Michael is 13 years old with a spelling age of around 9 years but who can read well and cope with all the curriculum areas. After analysing his attempts (plus looking through his school books) the following conclusions were made:

- he writes very quickly but can read his own writing;

- he can generalise visually in order to cope with unknown words (eg his spelling of the words 'hele(copter)' and 'sight' from knowing 'television' and 'height');

- he has acquired a wide sight vocabulary of known words;

- he can 'hear' letters that he misses out of words when he goes over his errors;

- he has problems with syllabication and has his own ideas of seeing ways of splitting up words for learning purposes;

- he can use his intelligence for attempting some words;

- there are some problems with letter order and sequencing;

- because of probable gaps in his phonic/phonemic learning he has missed out 'sound' letter patterns.

It was decided that he could cope with learning about the structure of words, such as prefixes, suffixes and word derivations so such a programme was set up.

*Late one night my firend woke me saing would you enjoy a trail run in my new helecopter. I had scaresle scurmbled into my tracsuite before we were away. The ligths of the sitty gloed benith the stars above. I was beging to wonder about are distinasion when I cought sight of the sping nife edght and the surface of what must of been a tipe of flying surcer wisling round us. We doghed skillfully to advoud an acided To are relif the space cared regained hight and we sanked down to earth and the curable bed I had neaver actaly lefted*

---

*Writing (including handwriting)*

If the pupil is able to write a sustained piece of work it can be useful for a 5–20-minute story or equivalent piece of writing to be analysed. Many skills can be observed such as:

- spellings;

- word usage;

- sentence construction;

- punctuation;

- amount of words attempted;

- presentation (including organisational skills).

---

*An example of a child with spelling and handwriting problems*

Steven is 11 years old with a history of spelling and fine motor control difficulties. He is left-handed and also has problems with spatial awareness. He works with an occupational therapist in order to help his hand control. He can learn words visually and he understands serial probability but he scans right to left and cannot pick out similar letter patterns in lists of words.

Example 1 at CA 7 years 3 months

Example 2 at CA 8 years 4 months

---

33

Example 3 at CA 9 years 10 months

I like siwning because if you ate hot. it cools you down and we do nice things in siwning I can siwn a 100 metters and I can do all the stroks. The olny one I can not do is Butfly

Example 4 at CA 11 years 1 month

I like Siwning Because if you ate hot it cools you downard we do nice thing in Siwning. I can siw a 100 Mtbers and I can do all the the stokes. The dny one I can not do is Butterfly.

It was originally felt that he may need to learn keyboard skills for word processing if his handwriting remained such a problem. However, after the final check it was felt that the handwriting programme was being successful and that he would be able to cope with the written work that was demanded in school. Where spelling is concerned he should work on visual patterning within words.

However, in order to analyse handwriting correctly the teacher has to observe the pupil actually writing. This is because it is important to check the following:

- handedness;

- pencil hold;

- position when writing;

- position of the book or piece of paper;

- letter formation.

The above criteria-reference assessments can evolve over time. What is needed is that where a particular problem is found the teacher should try to see where this problem starts so that a programme is built from the earliest stage of difficulty. All information should be carefully recorded.

## Standardised assessment

Assessments under this heading are those that have been given to a large number of the school population of varying ages in order to gain measured norms, standardised scores, percentiles or ages. Children's performances at tasks, such as reading and spelling, can be compared against those of their peers. General cognitive ability can also be measured. It has to be accepted that some standardised assessments are old and, therefore, norms might have changed over time. Scores from tests such as these should be sensitively taken into consideration.

### Early years identification

Early identification using standardised assessment where specific learning difficulties is concerned is in its infancy but research is being undertaken by educationists. One such example is through the work of Dr Chris Singleton at Hull University.

Singleton's work, named KEYSTAGE 1 CoPS, has been set up in order to tackle the problem of identification early in the child's life rather than waiting for the child to fail which might come much later in his or her educational career.

KEYSTAGE 1 CoPS is a computer programme of various sub-tests for use with 5-year-olds on an individual basis in order to attempt to ascertain which children may experience problems with reading later on in their school life. From the profile printout teachers can see which of these pupils may have an associated specific or dyslexic problem. His programme is not intended for labelling young children as 'dyslexic'. Rather the results will give a graphic profile of the child's cognitive strengths and weaknesses so that individual learning programmes can be devised and administered. Also it is intended that help can be given to eliminate the difficulty at an early stage, in fact before problems in the actual reading progress are experienced. So far encouraging results are being shown. (This research work is intended to be extended to programmes for older children as well.)

### Standardised assessment in the primary and secondary sectors
### Non-verbal performance testing

Group tests have been devised to look at this area of children's performance. Many of these are published by NFER.

There are fewer opportunities for individual assessment in this area. One of these is Ravens Progressive Matrices which is said to be a test of observation and clear thinking with two separate tests of matching patterns (Ravens Coloured Progressive Matrices for children up to 11 years and Raven's

Standard Progressive Matrices for 6 years up to adults). It is an untimed test so this is an advantage for children who need time to think things out. It does not give an IQ score although it provides information on a pupil's ability to think clearly and logically.

### Verbal performance testing

Also within the batteries of group tests are verbal assessments. Again information can be gained from NFER, and again there are fewer which assess on an individual basis.

As part of the Raven's Matrices there are also vocabulary scales (Crichton and Mill Hill Vocabulary Scales) which provide information on the pupil's ability to give word definitions. They are essentially oral assessments and, therefore, they complement the matrices tests. There can be interesting differences between the scores on the two sets of tests.

Another individual assessment of language is the British Picture Vocabulary Scales which is an assessment of the individual's received language or understanding of given words. The pupil is presented with many pages containing four pictures on each and the tester gives one word (either a label or concept) and the pupil has to point to what is known to be or thought to be the correct picture. Scores are given as standardised and percentile scores and age equivalents can be given. It is said that scores on this test often correlate well with the Verbal IQ score on the WISC tests.

### Reading tests

Standardised tests of reading are very varied. They can be group or individual assessments and can range from single word tests through to sentence and passage reading assessments. Some are now quite old and because reading tests are used in different ways it is most important to read the manuals before use. Reading tests can give information on reading ages, standardised scores or percentile ranks. Sometimes it may be felt to be necessary to show the discrepancy between actual age and reading age. This is particularly so if one wishes to match the readability and interest levels of reading books with the reader. However, it is more important to analyse how a reader accesses the text (see below for an explanation of miscue analysis).

### Passage reading

A miscue analysis of how a child reads can be accomplished through the passage reading tests such as the Revised Neale, the New Reading Analysis (readability 6.9 onwards) and the Individual Reading Analysis (for the early years reader). These tests are a set of graded passages which do not produce a reading age but a range of two scores between which the reader's competence at reading lies. The passages are not meant to be read without the tester noting how the pupil accesses the passages as a miscue exercise.

There are also comprehension questions which produce scores showing how the reader understands the texts. The Neale tests require these questions to be answered from memory which can either throw light on a pupil's memory capabilities or can give a false indication of the pupil's underlying ability if the pupil has a very poor retentive auditory memory but fundamentally excellent understanding. Testers should be aware of this when using this test on pupils with specific learning difficulties who have particular problems with their working memories. The other two assessments allow the pupils to refer back to the passages which give the tester indications of whether the pupil uses study skills of skimming, scanning, re-reading or use of picture clues.

---

*An example of a miscue analysis for the Individual Reading Analysis X (the first three passages)*

Kenny is 8 years 2 months and it is very difficult to help him acquire the skills for reading because he has very poor visual and auditory memories.

The house was dark.

The man went in.
    *men*
He    did        not come out.
*His/he b/d-id/did*

Pat    has    an old book.
*Pet/Pat heard        boot/d-ook*
She looks at it when she is    sad.
                *w-h-em    was*

The ship        was in dock.
    *sh-ip/ship        doot/dook/dop.*
A girl    ran on to the    deck.
    *g/girl r    in    a/the beek/beck/beach.*
She hid in a big box
            *book*
and was still there when the ship left.
    *sht                lit/la*

Kenny has gaps with his keyword knowledge and he has some visual directional confusion. He has some knowledge of reading for meaning and some rudimentary knowledge of phonic decoding. Although these passages were too difficult he did not give up. Because it seems that he could cope more easily with phonics a simple phonic programme is being set up.

---

*An example of a miscue analysis for the New Reading Analysis (the third passage from A)*

Jenny is 9 years old and reading has always been a problem for her.

It was late at night and Alex was on her way home. The roads were

silent and empty and all the houses were dark. It was then she heard a
*str        emp*
tremendous noise above her. Alex looked up into the night sky. She
*tend        nose  about*
could hardly believe her eyes. Some kind of huge aircraft was hovering
*couldn't hear bel                kid      hung air                hoving*
above the town. It had flashing lights in many different colours. What
*about                        flashed                much*
she saw next she would remember all her life.
*wouldn't                        left*

Problems arise from four areas:
- sight memory for core words and other high-interest words is still limited (she was more able to read keywords out of context)

- a visual reader who generalises from the shape of the word or part of the word

- her poor sight recall prevents efficient use of context

- has some simple phonic decoding strategies (and is more confident decoding out of context).

It was decided that Jenny should read just at her independent reading level to give her fluency. Simple cloze procedure should be given to help her understand guesswork. Activities for core word retention such as 'find the word' will be supplied, the phonic programme will be continued and she will be encouraged to use this knowledge when she reads texts.

## *Miscue analysis*

There are different approaches for teachers to take when undertaking a miscue analysis. For some it is helpful to note down in writing exactly what the child tries (as the above examples show) and then these can be analysed into the various strengths and weaknesses the child might have. From this information teaching programmes can be devised or altered. It can be advantageous if the passages are photocopied or marking sheets are used (as are supplied with these reading tests) for ease of recording. Also there are ways of using symbols which indicate how the reader attempted unknown words (such as 'sc' for 'self-correction' and circling any omitted word). Books listed in the References and Further Reading give examples of these.

Miscue analysis can only occur if the passages read are sufficiently demanding but not at frustration level where too many words are out of the child's knowledge. It can be more difficult to miscue when the child is reading his or her reading book because it would be hoped that this is at an appropriate level where only a few words are unknown. Some schools have banks of reading passages at varying readability levels which they will use half-termly with those pupils experiencing reading problems. In that way difficulties with texts are not associated with stories in books.

## *Single word reading*

It is sometimes helpful to ascertain how a pupil copes with individual words. In order to be successful on such tests a pupil either has to know the words from sight or has to use phonic or generalisation/analogy skills in order to work out the unknown word. If pupils have problems with word–sound associations or with decoding and synthesising then individual word assessments like the NFER Graded Word Reading Assessment can be used to help with this information.

*An example of how a pupil misread single words on the NFER-NELSON GRADED WORD READING TEST*
*Word Card 1*

Fay is 11 years 4 months and there is some concern about her strategies for coping with unknown words. It is felt that her language knowledge is average.

The first 10 words were correct.

| barrow | bought | ridiculous | friction | critical |
|--------|--------|-----------|----------|----------|
| *borrow* | *brought* | *right/righteousness* | | *ritual* |
| | | | | |
| phantom | enraged | cubicle | relish | antiseptic |
| *plantom* | *enrage* | *cabile* | *relidge* | *antisipatic* |
| | | | | |
| influenza | symmetrical | pedantic | vagrancy | client |
| *infludent* | *sImetri* | *ped* | *van* | *silent* |

futile

*futil* (short 'u')

Fay is a visual reader who generalises from the shape of the word and who seems content to pronounce 'non-words'. There are some signs of former phonic decoding skills but she needs to learn how to break down multi-syllabic words and use competent strategies in synthesising them. It was felt that this could be organised through textual reading and from the errors which came from this.

*Spelling tests*

There are few recent spelling tests which give spelling ages and as with reading, although it is sometimes helpful to see the discrepancy between the pupil's actual age and spelling age, it is more helpful to use spelling assessments as diagnostic tools. Two examples of spelling tests which give spelling ages are Schonell Spelling Test and Young Parallel Spelling.

An example of a pupil's spelling when given the Schonell Spelling Test
Di is 11 years 1 month and is being assessed at the beginning of her first term in the secondary school.

The first 30 words were spelt correctly.

| sight | mouth | large | might | brought |
|---|---|---|---|---|
| *site* | | *larged/large* (sc) | *mite* | *bought* |
| mistake | pair | while | skate | stayed |
| *misstake/mistake* (sc) | *paer/pear* | *wiyal/wieal* | | |
| yolk | island | nerve | join | fare |
| *yowck/yowk* | | | | *fair* |
| iron | health | direct | calm | headache |
| | *heath* | *b/diret/dierct* | *carm* | *headack* |
| | | *dieract* | | |

Di seems to be using visual approaches where spelling is concerned. Although her spelling is fairly competent it was decided to put her into the school's spelling programme which would give her some awareness of phonemic letter strings.

**Psychologist's Assessment**

Chartered educational psychologists either employed by the LEA or as private consultants usually administer the BAS (British Abilities Scale) or the WISC-R or WISC III (Wechsler Intelligence Scale for Children) battery of assessments in order to ascertain the child's cognitive ability.

The BAS is comprised of a number of sub-tests which assess various areas of cognitive performances. The WISC assessments are divided into two sections. One set of sub-tests makes up the Verbal IQ while the other set of sub-tests makes up the Performance IQ. The Full-scale IQ is based on scores from both sections.

Often children with specific learning difficulties have spiky profiles in that they score well on some sub-tests and poorly on others. Some psychologists and others concerned with dyslexia will look at the scores on four of the sub-tests, arithmetic, coding, information and digit span (which is termed the ACID profile) and if these are low in comparison with the other sub-test scores then it is felt that the child may be dyslexic. However, because children with specific learning difficulties differ in their intellectual profiles one should be wary of just using this information because the ACID profile is not always typical of a child with specific learning difficulties.

---

*An example of a child's sub-test scores from the Wechsler Intelligence Scale for Children III Edition*

Martin was 7 years 7 months when this was given.

Verbal IQ 127 Centile 96                    Performance IQ 97 Centile 42

| | | | |
|---|---|---|---|
| Information | 12 | Picture Completion | 13 |
| Similarities | 18 | Picture Arrangement | 8 |
| Arithmetic | 9 | Block Design | 10 |
| Vocabulary | 18 | Coding | 8 |
| Comprehension | 15 | Symbol Search | 10 |

The conclusions were:
- above average for age for verbal ability;

- verbal reasoning, vocabulary and comprehension all excellent;

- significant discrepancy between verbal and performance scores which can lead to difficulties where self-organisation is concerned;

- dyslexic features present in terms of weak working memory and slow processing of symbolic information. Visual sequencing skills are also weak;

- specific learning difficulties are affecting acquisition of literacy skills.

Recommendations:
- extra support with self-organisation in class;

- acknowledgement of short-term memory difficulties and strategies given to help him process and carry out instructions;

- multi-sensory teaching to improve his reading and spelling attainments.

---

Educational psychologists are also able to use the assessment findings to predict the child's probable learning potential in reading and spelling and will work out how significant in statistical terms are the differences between measured cognitive ability and reading and spelling attainment scores. These measures supply evidence when requests for statutory assessment under the *Code of Practice's* criteria are sent in to LEAs.

SENCOs should be able to interpret and explain psychologists' reports to parents, especially when parents feel that the numbers written down (IQ scores, potential scores, significance levels, spelling and reading ages) are more important than the diagnostic approach to assessment.

### The *Code of Practice* and Requests for Statutory Assessment

When a request is presented to the LEA for consideration for statutory assessment, the *Code of Practice* outlines four areas which deal with the evidence required (para. 3:61). The first two, concerning the National Curriculum attainments and results of cognitive and other standardised tests, have been dealt with above.

In paragraph 3.61. iii, the *Code* mentions some of the other factors which may be present when a pupil has specific rather than general learning difficulties. These are:

- Evidence of clumsiness is mentioned but whether this is in the area of gross motor control or fine motor control is not apparent. Evidence has to be both 'clear' and 'recorded'.

- Sequencing and visual perceptual difficulties are next referred to. This could mean that the pupil cannot sequence events as in story sequencing or that they find it difficult to spell words by writing the letters in the correct order (eg 'freind/friend' or 'littel/little'). Where visual perceptual difficulties are concerned they may find it hard to match similar words or they write letters and/or numbers with incorrect inversions and orientations.

- The phrase 'deficiencies in working memory' is written next. As has been already stated earlier in this book, the working memory is very important in that this underpins basic skills learning.

- 'Significant delays in language functioning' is the last factor mentioned. It is not clear whether this means receptive or expressive language but one can see that if a pupil's specific learning difficulties include language problems then he or she may have problems with the speaking and listening areas of the English National Curriculum and also that there will be other areas of the curriculum which will suffer because of language problems.

There are omissions in this section as some of the earlier mentioned performance indicators could be added. LEAs will probably work out their own set of extra criteria. However, it is felt by many educationists that this set of criteria should be shown as additional rather than being obligatory.

Part iv, the last in this section, deals with the emotional/behavioural problems which are said to be 'sometimes associated with specific learning difficulties'. Evidence is requested from: 'clear, recorded examples of withdrawn or disruptive behaviour, an ability to concentrate, or signs that the child experiences considerable frustration or distress in relation to his or her learning difficulties'. It is suggested that the LEA should see whether the evidence of the problem behaviours occur in those classes which require reading and writing.

Anyone who works with pupils with specific learning difficulties tries very hard to maintain the pupils' high self-esteem and positive attitudes. One should not expect a child to suffer from feelings of failure and worry or to start behaving unacceptably before the LEA decides to look into whether or not to start statutory assessment. Once again this should not be an obligatory requirement.

# Classroom Strategies at Stages 1–3

The *Code of Practice* suggests that schools follow the three-staged process for any child with a special educational need. Teachers working through these stages will use them to produce evidence of the problems and in-school ways of supporting and helping the pupil overcome them.

### Stage 1: The Class Teacher and Differentiation

Stage 1 is involved with gathering basic information about the child's specific learning problem after either a parent and/or teacher has expressed an initial concern. A first assessment of the problem will be made by the class teacher or tutor and 'special help within the normal curriculum framework, exploring ways in which increased differentiation of classwork' will be provided. The child's progress will be monitored and reviewed. Parents should be kept informed at all stages and their advice and help asked for.

Class teachers in the primary school, especially in the early years, can use the lists already mentioned if they find that there is a pupil who seems unable to cope with the demands of the classroom.

Class teachers in the upper end of the primary school and secondary subject teachers will either have been given information about which pupils have specific learning difficulties before they teach the particular child or they will have queries about those pupils who appear to be finding the subject difficult. There are the factors to check from the lists previously given or this preliminary question can be posed in order to decide whether differentiated work is necessary:

- are all the pupils acquiring the skills and knowledge that are intended from the particular lesson?

In order to answer that question, the teachers will have to check from:

- how the pupils answer orally;

- how the pupils react/function in whatever way they are requested;

- how the pupils appear to be listening;

- how the pupils produce written work;

- what is their general behaviour within the lesson.

This should give information which can be acted upon. Teachers could either immediately differentiate materials and/or change their own input to the lessons or the pupils' output. They could also share information with other members of staff to see if similar reactions occur in other lessons. Or they could contact the SENCO for extra support.

Differentiation can affect the way the teacher delivers the curriculum, the materials used, the organisational structure within the learning situation and the way the individual is able to access what is being taught and expected of him or her.

Young children can be grouped quite easily and those with literacy skills given work adapted to their needs either with the class teacher or with a classroom support assistant.

Before the more formalised approach to teaching reading and spelling is undertaken, work on early language skills should be given. These are detailed in books such as *Learning Difficulties in Reading and Writing – A*

*Teacher's Manual* by Reason and Boot. Also, ideas for activities and games can be found in the series of games and activity books for reading, spelling and language produced by NASEN, among others. Much of the differentiated work in early years classes should be oral so that phonological awareness is built up and so that the pupils are able to cope with sequencing and discrimination skills in both the auditory and the visual modes.

Young children may need to make their own reading books or have these made for them. They will need to read and reread repetitive stories which they can memorise. Ideas for home–school liaison where reading is concerned can be found in *Teachers and Parents: Together for Reading* (NASEN). They may need someone to scribe their news and simple stories or to use sequencing techniques when words are written on sticky-backed cards.

As it will be noticed, the suggested differentiated approach for children with suspected specific learning difficulties in the early years is no different from that for children with suspected general learning difficulties.

As children grow older and the work in the classroom becomes more demanding then differentiated work can be matched to individual needs. In brief, children with recording problems may be allowed to use alternative methods such as producing diagrams and drawings or by one-word labelling. Tape recorders and/or word processing can be helpful. If reading is the concern then taped information might be provided, or worksheets might be rewritten to match the readability of the learner. Organisational and memory problems can be helped by *aide-mémoires*, instructions given as written memos or the learner not given an overload for retention purposes (short sentences used with repetition on behalf of both the teacher and the learner).

What has to be remembered is that children with specific learning difficulties, like any child with a special educational need, have the right to a broad, balanced curriculum and if they have problems in any particular area help must be given to alleviate these. Although differentiation is mentioned as the strategy for help under Stage 1, it is implicit that differentiation has to be used during the other stages or whenever a child has problems with curriculum access.

---

*An example of a pupil placed on Stage 1*

Sally at 8 years 10 months was placed on Stage 1 because of parental concern about her reading and spelling attainments. It was noted that much absence had hindered her learning and she also changed schools at Key Stage 1. Glasses were recently prescribed. The class teacher checked Sally's reading on Salford B Sentence Reading Test and she scored a

---

reading age of 7 years 10 months and her spelling scored at 7.1 years on Schonell Spelling Test. Sally's strengths were visual and although she knew her basic phonic skills she did not use them in her reading.

In class she read daily to an ancillary who encouraged her to use phonic decoding and contextual strategies when she found she did not sight-recognise a word. Sally also worked in class with a small group of other pupils on a structured spelling programme.

At 9 years 10 months Sally was using all strategies within her reading which had increased to 9 years 2 months on Salford C and her spelling had improved to 7 years 10 months on Schonell. The programme was seen to have worked.

## Stage 2: The Involvement of the SENCO

Stage 2 is triggered either by the Stage 1 review where it is felt that the pupil needs more assessment or after the initial concern where it is felt that early intensive action is required. The SENCO is involved at this stage. Here some of the assessment procedures mentioned above would be necessary so that a more diagnostic profile of the child could be built up and a learning programme devised. This would be written onto an Individual Education Plan (IEP) which would be carried out, reviewed and monitored (see IEPs and Specific Learning Difficulties).

## Stage 3: The Involvement of a 'Specialist'

This is a very similar situation to Stage 2 except that here external 'specialists', such as educational psychologists and members of LEA advisory and support services, become involved. These educationists may carry out observations and more detailed assessments in order to give additional ideas for a teaching and learning programme which would be written onto the IEP. Similar reviews and monitoring of this programme would take place.

*An example of a pupil placed on Stage 3 with reference to possible request for statutory assessment*

After school monitoring and support, Liam was moved to Stage 3 at CA 9 years 3 months and both an advisory teacher and an LEA educational psychologist became involved with assessments and planning learning programmes. After the first review when Liam was 10 years 1 month it was felt that there was enough evidence to request statutory assessment.

- IQ was at the average level (WISC Full Score 96) with his non-verbal abilities slightly higher than his verbal abilities whereas his attainments in reading and spelling were particularly weak. As measured on Salford Sentence Reading Test C his reading age was 6.8 years (a probable overestimate as he could not score on MIRA X). On Schonell Spelling Test his spelling age was 6.0 years;

- visual perception was very weak;

- visual and auditory memories were particularly limited;

- concentration span was limited and he could both be distracted and cause distraction if confronted with work he could not cope with. He needed much individual help;

- the school had helped him access the curriculum by differentiating as much as possible;

- structured programmes of work as suggested by the LEA advisory staff were carried out within the school by his class teacher and learning support staff (This was learning keywords for reading and spelling, reading Trog books with 'easier' extra books written by the advisory teacher, doing oral work on sounds but not beginning more formal phonic work until some individual help could be provided);

- parental involvement and backup of work at home is carried out.

Liam's case was discussed by the LEA panel and a statutory assessment was initiated.

## In-Class or Out-of-Class Programmes at Stages 2 and 3

It is expected that work programmes from the IEPs would be carried out in the normal classroom setting, but there may be times when small group or individual teaching would be appropriate. This type of organisation would depend on the staffing of particular schools and whether there were extra support staff, either teachers or support assistants, who could be allocated to undertake this work. Liaison with parents is most important here.

Larger primary schools and secondary schools may find it easier to group-teach children with learning problems. If extra literacy support is to be given there is then always the dilemma of which subject areas could be 'missed'. Also from an organisational point of view it could seem expedient to teach pupils with specific literacy difficulties alongside those with problems of a more generalised nature. However, because of the former's particular needs and the latter's probable slower rate of learning, from an educational point of view this is not the most advantageous way of working.

There are programmes published for group work which if used as stated could be beneficial for children with specific learning difficulties. Examples of these are *Letterland, Alpha to Omega, Attack* and *Spelling Made Easy* for spelling and *Distar* for reading. Reading schemes such as *Wellington Square* and *Crown* are frequently used but it should be remembered that these were not written particularly for those with specific learning difficulties.

*Multi-sensory teaching approaches*

Individualised programmes are various which purport to be multi-sensory (and a brief explanation of a multi-sensory teaching approach can be found below) and which endeavour to find ways of tackling reading, spelling, handwriting and organisational problems. An often used programme is the multi-sensory language course that Kathleen Hickey devised. Many of these can begin in the primary sector and continue into the secondary sector because of their cumulative learning approach. It is important that for many pupils these programmes, as well as being multi-sensory, should be well-structured, sequential and contain a phonic component.

Because children with specific learning difficulties have problems with auditory and visual sequencing, with synthesising of stored information and with working memory, it can be difficult to use solely a visual or an auditory method when teaching literacy skills. Even combining these may not succeed because the extra sensory systems of tactile-kinaesthetic (using touch and action) are required in order to produce the multi-sensory approach.

This approach co-ordinates the interaction of the senses of seeing, hearing, speaking and doing. It integrates the pupil's visual, auditory, oral and kinaesthetic capabilities. Programmes using these methods start at the base line of the child's knowledge which is why detailed assessment is necessary in order to determine what the child can or cannot do. The teaching programme then builds on this knowledge slowly and cumulatively. Each newly learnt process has to be thoroughly gone over until it becomes an automatic process. Once this occurs, the next stage in the structured process can be taught.

As well as detailed assessment procedures being undertaken before the programme starts, it is also important to record everything that is taught and learnt and periodically to revisit past processes to see that these have not been forgotten. It is essential not to rush any stage in the learning and, therefore, it is fundamental to let both the pupil and the parents understand why such programmes are being used.

---

*A basic example of learning through a multi-sensory approach: Acquisition of letter names and sounds*

It can be seen that the processes overlap and are not intended to be carried out as separate functions.

1. The particular letter to be taught will be named and given its usual sound by the teacher. The child will listen using his or her aural processes.

2. By looking at the shape of the letter he or she will bring visual processes into play.

3. He or she will repeat the name and sound (thus again listening), so working in the oral mode.

4. A wooden or plastic letter shape can be felt using the tactile approach.

5. The pupil can write or make the letter shape employing the kinaesthetic mode (again saying the name and sound).

These five processes will help to fix the name and the sound and how to write the particular letter into the memory.

---

Words for reading and spelling can be dealt with similarly. The teacher will write and say the word which will be looked at and repeated. Plastic or wooden letters can be used to make the word with the cue and then without the cue. The whole word or even the separate letters can be spoken while this is happening. In the end the child writes the correct word on cue or reads it when it is presented.

If the identified problems are not as basic or entrenched to need total multi-sensory approaches then modifications to the above can be made. As has been stated teaching should always try to match the child's strengths and weaknesses. Therefore, they will reinforce and consolidate what is known and thus become a positive reinforcement to the learning situation. They will augment what is not known in order to develop what could be the problem areas. In this way children with problems in the visual or auditory modes can be taught more easily through the preferred manner and can have the area where there is uncertainty and problems built up as a supplement.

The maxim to follow is to know the problem areas in as much detail as possible and to match the teaching and learning requirements to them.

**Literacy Skills Teaching**

There is no particular order for teaching literacy skills with individuals or small groups if teachers are to devise the programme themselves. (Published programmes have their own particular sequences.) However, one could look at the following to determine where to begin such a programme.

*Reading*

- Teaching of common core sight words (eg the 250 McNally and Murray keywords) *These can be taught as flash cards, on probes, in sentences or found within other types of reading material;*

- the building up of sight vocabulary (high interest or subject specific words) *Structured reading schemes can be used (eg Wellington Square or Crown) or particular words pertaining to a subject area can be taught as whole word entities;*

- the acquisition of reading techniques such as contextual cueing, reading on and returning, cloze procedure;

- teaching of letter sounds and phonic decoding *(working through the short vowels and consonant-vowel-consonant words, to consonant digraphs and blends, to regular endings such as 'ink/and/ent' etc, to words with the modifying 'e' ending, to common vowel digraphs such as 'ar/or/er' and more irregular vowel digraphs such as 'ow/ou/au' and harder units of sound such as 'ought/ight/ear/air' );*

- structured phonic-based reading schemes can be used (such as *Fuzzbuzz*);

- multi-syllabic word attack skills *(including syllabication and the understanding and synthesising of syllables and knowledge of prefixes and suffixes);*

- higher reading skills *(such as reading for meaning, reading between and beyond the lines, skimming, scanning, researching).*

*Spelling*

- sight word spelling of common core words *(using the visual approach advocated by Peters and Cripps in 'Catchwords' operating the methods of Look, Remember, Cover, Write, Check plus Say in order to cover all the senses in a multi-sensory approach and/or Simultaneous Oral Spelling techniques, see Appendix 5);*

- phonemic spelling strategies *(using letters and letter combinations to attempt unknown words);*

- understanding serial probability *(which letters can be used together in the English spelling system and checking the phonemic attempts with visual memory for self-correction);*

- proofreading and dictionary skills *(which could include the use of the specialised ACE Dictionary and Spellmasters and/or spellcheckers on word processors).*

*Handwriting*

- correct letter formation *(coupled with holding the writing instrument correctly and sitting in an appropriate position);*

- cursive writing.

*Written work*

- generation of ideas and being able to use these to write a beginning, the body of the text and a conclusion. (Some tips for this can be found in *Learning to Learn* published by NASEN);

- correct punctuation and grammatical accuracy.

If teachers are able to work out the individual programmes then they are not tied to anything published and can, therefore, meet the needs of the particular pupil.

## The *Code of Practice* and Teaching Requirements

The *Code of Practice* makes some statements about what type of teaching should have been carried out if a request for statutory assessment is made by a school for a particular pupil. This is found in 3:62 under the heading 'The child's special educational provision'.

The first section appears to be more secondary-oriented as it talks about making the curriculum and the school day accessible by letting all teachers know about the child's particular needs (see Appendix 1 for a check-sheet for subject teachers). It goes on to deal with how appropriate practices should be adopted for the child to record information, that the school should have appropriate marking policies and that devices such as personal dictionaries should be used. This matches what has been briefly said on differentiation.

The next section is more prescriptive and relevant to both the primary and secondary sectors. External experts should have been asked to help with the formulation of the IEPs which should have been closely monitored and fully evaluated. Examples of what should have been written on these state:

- **'for reading:** a reading programme structured to respond to the child's particular strengths and weaknesses as revealed by a diagnostic assessment of the child's reading performance, and including phonics teaching;

- **'for spelling:** a structured spelling support programme promoted and monitored by teachers across the curriculum, such as simultaneous oral spelling linked to the development of cursive writing;

- **'the use of multi-sensory teaching strategies:** directed to developing the basic skills of reading, spelling, or number.'

These suggestions have been dealt with above.

## Support in the Secondary Classroom

This support work can be carried out by support assistants, members of the special needs department, subject specialists who have been given special needs responsibility and members of staff who have time on their timetables. Unless this support is given specifically for a pupil with specific learning difficulties who has a statement then help is often spread around all pupils who have learning difficulties. Subject teachers should be made aware that these two categories of pupils learn in different ways and at different rates and that grouping them together may not be the best type of organisation. The pupil with specific learning difficulties should be an integral member of the class but his or her particular problems should be known and noted.

Pupils with specific learning difficulties can be assisted in the following ways:

- worksheets can be specially prepared to take account of particular problems;

- specialised or technical vocabulary can be taught prior to the lesson (both reading and spelling);

- help can be made available with the organisation of written work (eg mind-mapping, brainstorming, webbing);

- preparation of written and/or tape-recorded notes can occur;

- the facility can be organised for the pupil to tape-record information;

- transcribing from the pupil's dictation and/or help writing up the tape-recorded information can be provided;

- the facility can be organised for the pupil to word process and be helped with this (tuition and support);

- direct teaching, if appropriate, can be given to help with understanding and learning particular skills and concepts for the subject.

---

*An example of a secondary-aged pupil with a statement of special educational needs who is well able to give his own perceptions of his problems and his needs*

Sam is 13 years 4 months and at an Annual Review said that his problems were:

- he had difficulties in all aspects of written work because of only being able to write extremely slowly (both in school and for homework). Copying from the board was particularly difficult as he was too slow to finish what he should do;

---

- in spelling he made many mistakes when he was writing information etc and not being able to concentrate on how to spell correctly;

- with self-organisation, as his memory was weak (already he had lost two locker keys);

- in speed reading, because although he can read quite competently he cannot skim and scan;

- with maths, as although he felt he knew how to cope with certain aspects he was too slow and things took a while to sink into his brain;

- with concern about future examinations, as he does not think he will cope at GCSE level with all subjects. He feels that A-level work will be easier.

Sam's strategies so far include using a small tape-recorder for both homework and classwork but this makes him appear different from his peers. He uses a small Spellmaster and has access to a personal computer at home although as yet his keyboarding skills are not particularly good. He gets a lot of parental support.

It was felt that Sam also needed a personal weekly timetable setting out books/equipment for his daily lessons. Staff needed to be aware of his slow processing and to make allowances for this. Wherever possible he would be given copies of notes rather than being expected to copy these himself and while others were employed with this he would be given extra time for completion of classwork. They would also check his homework diary to see that he had the correct information. He was allocated one lesson of support teaching where the emphasis would be on higher reading skills, study skills, hints on how to write essays and projects. There would be some reinforcement of spelling 'rules'. At home help would be given with keyboarding skills.

## Special Provision in Examinations

Not all pupils with specific learning difficulties will need or even benefit from special provisions in public examinations. Nor is a statement of special educational need required before these are granted (at the time of writing this book). However, if it is felt that a pupil may not do him or herself justice in examinations then schools should look into requesting that special provisions are put into practice. Parents should also be involved in any discussion about the need for special provisions.

Some pupils will cope during lessons but not during examinations. Problems in spelling, reading fast enough to extract relevant information and writing fast enough to produce enough work may present the pupil with extra stress. Just to know that extra time will be allocated may alleviate these feelings.

A recognised educational psychologist is required to write a report for pupils who are deemed to have specific learning difficulties within a period of 18 months prior to the examinations. There is usually a standard form which has to be filled in although examination boards can differ in their requirements so schools via the examination officer or SENCO need to find out exactly what evidence is required to support any application for special provisions. Often what is needed is discrepancy between reading age and cognitive ability and reading and writing speeds. The assessment has to be carried out using standardised reading and spelling tests.

As well as extra time, up to 25 per cent extra, some pupils with specific learning difficulties may be entitled to an amanuensis (a scribe or reader), tape-recording, working on a word processor and concessions for poor spelling. However, it has to be proved that the pupil's main mode of working is dictating or word processing if that is the provision requested.

The final certificate will be endorsed if the examination board has not been able to judge the spelling, punctuation and grammar of the individual which would occur if an amanuensis was used. It would have to be decided by both the pupil and parents if this was a preferred option.

## IEPs and Specific Learning Difficulties

Individual Education Plans are requirements for Stages 2 and 3 and for the pupil who has a statement of special educational need. These are documents which outline the child's problems by stating long-term goals and short-term targets in order to help overcome these. When writing IEPs teachers have to state who will carry out the teaching programme and what materials and/or methods will be used. A review date has to be stated and the parents should know what the plans are.

When filling in IEPs teachers should answer these key words:

- WHAT?      these are the particular targets that are stated for each pupil after assessment and consultation;

- HOW?  this would state the methods of teaching/supporting;

- WHICH?  this would state the materials to be employed;

- WHO?  the adult(s) involved (with parental liaison and backup);

- WHEN?  the day(s) of the week and the particular times;

- WHERE?  the room (either in or out of the classroom);

- WHAT?  the success criteria (in order to evaluate if the programme has been successful);

- HOW?  the method of recording progress made.

A hidden question, but one that needs to be kept at the back of the mind, is WHY? Answering this gives the rationale behind the IEP for the particular individual.

Sometimes teachers want to put too many targets into a programme and then find that it is not manageable and nothing gets completed satisfactorily. When writing targets the teacher should consider the following suggestions:

- do not state more than two targets in each skill area;

- do not try to work on more than is achievable (others can be added when the first are successful);

- use an active verb which is in the future tense;

- write the targets in factual objective terms;

- try to ensure that the targets can be achieved but make them challenging;

- try to make sure that the outcomes can be measured;

- relate outcomes to knowledge and skills;

- relate outcomes to the assessment criteria.

*An example of an Individual Education Plan for a child at Stage 3*

Stage 3: Individual Education Plan    Date opened: 14 September 1995

Name:   Danny W.
d.o.b. :   13 June 1986

Strengths: Verbally able, practical and artistic. Has a good grasp of general knowledge and has a lovely personality.

Concerns (attach previous IEPs and any other relevant information): Reading is improving but there are gaps in his decoding skills. Great problems with spelling, seems unable to remember core words or to see similarities in words with same patterns.

Long-term aims:     1. To teach him the more common word patterns which include vowel digraphs so that his reading reaches his age level.
2. To enable him to communicate with his written work.

| TARGETS | ACTION/PROGRAMME | SUCCESS CRITERIA |
| --- | --- | --- |
| 1. To teach him word endings such as 'ear/ain/out/own/ight' etc | Worksheets and word lists | 90% accuracy when working on the lists/use in unseen reading |
| 2. To spell correctly the three/four-letter words from the Keyword lists | Keyword lists with SOS and use of mnemonics | 80% accuracy when reviewed |
| 3. To use appropriate sound–symbol correspondence when writing own words | Check knowledge of basic sounds – work on three-letter words (then with four, consonant digraphs and blends) – use multi-sensory approaches | Unknown words in own writing showing signs of phonemic structure |

Adults supporting the programme: School's support teacher working on 2/3 with backup from special needs support assistant. Class teacher working on 1. Parents backing up 2 and working on sound games (also hearing reading).

Time and place: Two 15-minute individual sessions on Mon./Thurs. with the support teacher – three 15-minute backup in class with the support assistant – daily reading to the class teacher – daily work at home.

LEA staff involved: LEA advisory teacher to review and advise.

Monitoring and review arrangements and date of next review: Advisory teacher to review in late Nov. School to monitor each month. Review with parents 10 December 1995.

**The Statement**

Reference to what evidence the *Code of Practice* expects schools to provide for the LEA if statutory assessment is requested has been given throughout the chapters of this book so far. In the *Code of Practice* 3:62, apart from the programmes of work offered to the pupil, the following are also required:

- through monitoring by external specialists there is evidence to support the fact that the pupil has not made significant progress as monitored on the structured programme and/or his or her level of attainment is falling behind the majority of children;

- parents have been fully involved;

- where it has been thought appropriate access to information technology has been given both at home and at school;

- any emotional and behavioural problems which may have been experienced by the pupil have been monitored and help has been provided to lessen any anxiety experienced and to enhance self-esteem;

- where appropriate and with the parents' consent advice from the school doctor and/or the child's general practitioner has been sought.

It can seem that there are a great many hurdles to jump over before a statutory assessment is initiated and LEAs will have their own additional criteria and basis for who should qualify for a statement. The balance of evidence presented has to show that the child's specific learning difficulties are significant and/or complex and ideas on this will differ from LEA to LEA. It has to be determined that the measures taken to help the child within school have not had the desired effect and, therefore, extra special educational provision over and above that which reasonably could be expected from the school is required.

LEAs are required to set up a moderating group in order to ensure that the evidence received from schools leads to consistent administration of which pupils are allocated a statement of special educational needs. They may also require certain LEA staff to monitor those pupils with a statement of special educational needs to determine whether the allocated resources are being used effectively.

LEAs may determine additional criteria for ceasing to maintain a statement. This procedure might be suggested by the school and agreed to by the parents when the child no longer requires additional support and resources and can access the curriculum with relative ease. Or the LEA may set guidelines where LEA staff monitor and review a child's progress and when the child reaches a certain literacy level and has appropriate coping strategies there may be no further need for the statement to be maintained. It would be hoped that all former aspects of the pupil's difficulties would be reassessed rather than basing the criteria for destatementing on a single educational aspect, such as reading competency.

---

*An example of what might be written on a statement*

Part 2 describes the pupil's special educational needs with a short general descriptive account and some statements to identify the learning difficulties. (Quotations from the actual statement are set in italics.)

*Kevin is described as a boy with specific learning difficulties in terms of developing basic skills. He has poor auditory short-term memory skills and a poor visual memory which gives him problems in retaining sight words without constant reinforcement. Recent tests have indicated that Kevin functions intellectually at an average level and he is said to be quite creative. Kevin is also described as becoming increasingly withdrawn at school and his self-esteem is said to be low.*

*The LEA has identified Kevin's learning difficulties as follows:*
1. *poor auditory short-term memory skills which inhibit his ability to acquire basic literacy through a phonic approach;*
2. *weak visual memory skills which inhibit his ability to acquire literacy skills through visual channels;*
3. *low self-confidence and self-esteem.*

Part 3 which specifies the special educational provision is in three parts which state the objectives, the educational provision to meet needs and objectives, and monitoring arrangements.

The objectives translate the stated learning difficulties into long-term aims.

1. *to acquire a more complete and reliable phonic knowledge so as to develop his ability to read for information and enjoyment;*
2. *to develop and extend his sight vocabulary so as to help him become more accurate at reading;*
3. *to develop and extend his spelling skills so as to extend his ability to communicate effectively in writing;*
4. *to promote his confidence and enhance his self-esteem.*

The provision states what the school should provide with LEA support if this is specified. In Kevin's case this was an additional two hours' teaching support in order to carry out an intense, structured literacy programme. The provision section may also say that the advisory teachers should be consulted where necessary. The monitoring section sets out that the Individual Education Plan should be drawn up with appropriate short-term educational targets and should be sent to the parents and to the LEA. Monitoring and Annual Reviews have to be carried out.

## Whole School Policy

Chapter 2 of the *Code of Practice* covers the school-based stages of assessment and provision. In this chapter the duties of the governing bodies are stated and one of these is publicising the school policy on special educational needs (2:10).

About 20 per cent of children nationally may have some form of special educational need at some time in their school life and about 18 per cent of these will have their needs met in their mainstream schools. This leaves about 2 per cent for whom a statutory statement of special educational need may be necessary. It should be kept in mind that most of this remaining 2 per cent will be in specialised schooling. Of course, percentages will vary over LEAs and schools.

As it has been stated in the Introduction, the British Dyslexia Association gives percentages for those pupils suffering from specific learning difficulties which are 4 per cent having severe problems (or as they say about one in every class) and up to 10 per cent having some type of specific learning difficulty which would need attention.

Duties of governors can be found in NASEN's publication, *Governor's Guide to Special Educational Needs in Mainstream School* by Graham Bill. Other publications which deal with LEA, school and SENCO responsibilities are *A Primary School Approach* by Kathleen Luton and *A Secondary Approach* by Mike Gordon and Hazel Smith.

The parts of 2:10 in the *Code of Practice* which are particularly applicable to this publication are that the policy should include:

- any SEN specialism:
  it is becoming more common to find members of staff in schools having some extra qualification for the teaching of specific learning difficulties (eg RSA diploma/DI diploma/advanced diploma from universities) and it is important that use is made of this knowledge;

- identification and assessment arrangements, and review procedures:
  schools should be showing that there is a difference between specific and general learning difficulties and should be making appropriate arrangements (this is dealt with in the chapters Identification, Assessment and Classroom Strategies at Stages 1–3);

- the school's arrangements for SEN in-service training:
  if schools are to recognise and accept that specific learning difficulties are a separate section within the realm of special educational needs then staff as a whole need to be aware of the problems experienced by such pupils. Also, if individual members of staff want to acquire further specialist knowledge about specific learning difficulties they should be encouraged to undertake this and funding should be made available;

- use made of teachers and facilities from outside the school, including support services:
  LEAs differ in their provision of psychological services and support and advisory services but where there are LEAs providing particular 'experts' for specific learning difficulties these should be mentioned with reference as to how they are consulted and used;

- links with health and social services, educational welfare services and any voluntary organisation:
  there are voluntary bodies such as local Dyslexia Associations with whom schools may have contact. There may be a member of staff who is a member of such a body and relevant literature received should be shared.

Specific learning difficulties can be subsumed within the other parts of the policy where provision, access to the curriculum, integration and parental partnership are concerned.

Resourcing special educational needs comes from the school's budget. Some LEAs work out formulae for providing extra funding for those schools whose percentage of children with special educational needs are deemed to be greater than would normally be expected. Specific learning difficulties resourcing needs will have to be measured from within the overall budget and there will be organisational implications for dealing with individuals' problems. Examples of practice are given in Classroom Strategies at Stages 1–3 which show how both group and individual work can be carried out.

# Staff Development

Paragraph 2:26 in the *Code of Practice* deals with the aspect of in-service training of staff. It recommends that the school's SEN in-service training policy should be part of the ongoing school development plan and that where appropriate this should meet the needs of both teachers and support assistants.

### The Special Educational Needs Co-ordinator
The school should use the SENCO for in-school staff development but before this occurs he or she may have to be provided with some extra training. Some co-ordinators may have general additional qualifications in

special educational needs or may be equipped with a particular specialism but this might not cover specific learning difficulties. There are national courses which could be taken up. Some of these lead to further qualifications and some are of a shorter duration. Often these are organised by the RSA (Royal Society of Arts), British Dyslexia Association, the Dyslexia Institute, the Helen Arkell Centre or by education departments attached to universities. However, not all SENCOs would be able to undertake such training either because of the financial aspect or because of the travel and/or boarding implications. LEAs should mount courses for SENCOs dealing with the specific learning difficulties so that these staff members are:

- able to recognise the differences between a child with specific learning difficulties and one with general learning difficulties;

- aware of the additional problems children with specific learning difficulties may face (eg dyslexia, dyspraxia, dysgraphia, dyscalculia, dysphasia, Scotopic Sensitivity Syndrome, ADD);

- able to use appropriate identification and assessment procedures;

- able to advise on differentiated techniques within the classroom;

- knowledgeable about the materials available;

- knowledgeable about the teaching programmes available both for groups and individuals;

- able to advise on and write IEPs for Stages 2 and 3 which can be monitored;

- able to liaise with parents and formulate partnership approaches;

- able to co-ordinate all the relevant information required if a pupil is felt to need a statutory assessment;

- able to transfer the requirements of the statement onto an IEP;

- able to provide in-service training for the staff of their particular school.

Courses such as these should preferably lead to some kind of certification either from the LEA or validated from a college of higher education. They should be run by LEA staff who have appropriate qualifications or skills or by external specialists. It is not reasonable to expect SENCOs to undertake detailed courses such as these in twilight sessions. If LEAs are to recognise the needs of pupils with specific learning difficulties then release cover should be made available and SENCOs directed to attend. It may not be realistic for a co-ordinator from every school to be expected to attend such a course, for schools differ in size, especially those in the primary sector. It may be more relevant, therefore, to have courses such as the above mounted for the secondary SENCOs and one primary SENCO in a pyramid or cluster of schools. Then the training can be given to the other primary co-ordinators in a less 'formal' situation or as a rolling programme over the years.

If SENCOs have no additional expertise and/or training in special educational needs in general, these teachers should have a thorough knowledge of the processes of literacy development. Sessions for this should cover:

- the development and teaching of speaking and listening and how these influence the process of reading;

- the development of reading which would include
  - phonological awareness and the auditory skills
  - visual skills
  - word attack skills (including phonics, sight words and context)
  - multi-sensory approaches
  - higher reading skills
  - appraisal of published material
  - readability
  - assessment (including miscue analysis, sub-skills, standardised tests);

- the development of spelling which would include
  - auditory and visual processes
  - spelling stages
  - strategies for teaching spelling
  - appraisal of published material
  - assessment (including miscue analysis, sub-skills, standardised tests);

- the development of written work which would include
  - handwriting (including letter formation, legibility and flow, posture and pen hold and handedness)

- emergent writing
- higher writing skills.

It would be helpful if additional information was given about numeracy problems and the acquisition of mathematical concepts and processes. Also, it is important for teachers to know about learning styles and strategies for children to cope with their specific learning problems.

## The Special Needs Department Staff

The type of information and training needed for other members of staff would be different from that given to the SENCOs although there would be some similarities. Members of special needs departments would need information on:

- the differences between a child with specific learning difficulties and one with general learning difficulties;

- the use of appropriate identification and assessment procedures;

- the materials available;

- how to write IEPs for Stage 2 and how to monitor IEPs in Stages 2 and 3;

- the delivery of particular learning programmes.

This information could be disseminated in special needs department meetings either in their own school or with other support teachers in other schools. LEA advisory teachers could be called in to help with running the sessions if this is deemed necessary.

Support teachers and those working with children with literacy problems also need more generalised knowledge about literacy (and maybe numeracy) as outlined in the section for SENCOs.

## Class and Subject Teachers

Class and subject teachers should be given information about specific learning difficulties at least once a year. This could be given at a staff meeting and should be the responsibility of the SENCO. It is also advisable to update staff about actual individuals' problems. Where secondary staff are concerned it may be advisable to also give them a profile of individual children (see Appendix 1 for an example). Also in secondary schools it is sometimes easier for the SENCO to attend departmental meetings in order

66

to focus on the particular concerns of that curriculum area. Some secondary schools appoint 'link' members of staff from curriculum areas who meet regularly with the special needs department. Staff should be told about:

- the differences between a child with specific learning difficulties and one with general learning difficulties and be aware of the problems he or she may have in accessing the curriculum;

- how to organise differentiated techniques within the classroom;

- any materials available for helping children with specific learning difficulties within their classrooms;

- the use of IEPs for Stages 2 and 3 and how these should be monitored.

**Support Assistants**

Some schools require support assistants to undertake both supporting and teaching roles. Therefore, not only do these members of the school staff need to attend the staff meetings but they may also require some specialised in-service training. They need to be made aware of why they are carrying out a particular teaching programme and how they should record results. Many LEAs organise generalised courses for support assistants and very often these refer in particular to literacy and behavioural aspects. However, support assistants also need to understand the differences in learning approaches of the child with specific learning difficulties and the child with general learning difficulties. They also need some basic information about the processes of reading and spelling and why particular methods are used in teaching these literacy areas.

**Governors**

Governors also have in-service needs because of their duties where special educational needs are concerned (see the *Code of Practice* 2:6). If the school's policy is going to include particular sections about specific learning difficulties then the governors, in particular if there is a governor who has been given responsibility for special educational needs, should be aware of the different categories of special educational need which include specific learning difficulties. Often LEAs put special educational needs as an item for governors' training and within that there should be time allotted for a definition and explanation of specific learning difficulties.

### The LEA

Most schools work within the framework of an LEA and these local education authorities have different ways of meeting the needs of pupils with specific learning difficulties. There may be support teams of peripatetic teachers who work with children with literacy difficulties. Some authorities employ teachers who have specialist qualifications for specific learning difficulties who undertake in-school teaching programmes. Some authorities have specialist advisory teachers who assess and monitor children with difficulties at the more severe end of the specific learning difficulties continuum. There are, in some LEAs, specialist centres which work on a tutorial basis for literacy support while others provide special classes where pupils have intensive literacy help alongside other areas of the curriculum either within the class or in the mainstream of the host school.

Schools that have been given grant maintained status may also be able to use the services provided by their LEA by purchasing the support. These schools can also call upon other LEA teams or independent teams for advice.

### Independent Schools

If a pupil has very severe specific learning difficulties and it is deemed that he or she will take a long time to learn to acquire the processes for competent reading, or has attendant emotional/behavioural problems which are impeding learning, then some LEAs will fund day or residential placement in the independent school sector.

# Parents

The concept of parental partnership with schools is enshrined in the *Code of Practice* (sections 2:28–2:33) and parents' involvement in their child's education is given emphasis throughout the school's staged processes. This is carried on into the area of statutory assessment if appropriate.

Children's progress will be diminished if their parents are not seen as partners in the educational process with unique knowledge and information to impart. Professional help can seldom be wholly effective unless it builds upon parents' capacity to be involved and unless parents consider that professionals take account of what they say and treat their views and anxieties as intrinsically important.

(*Code of Practice*, para. 2:28)

Parents may be the initiators of the staged process. If they have any worries or if there is anxiety felt about their child having a specific learning difficulty, schools should treat these with concern and give them due attention. Parents should be given information about specific learning difficulties in understandable terms. Some may have already sought out such information from voluntary associations, have read articles from magazines and/or newspapers, have listened to radio programmes or have watched TV programmes. They may obtain mixed messages. Schools might feel that the child's specific learning problem is mild and can be coped with under a differentiated Stage 1 whereas outside independent advice has mentioned the necessity for statutory assessment leading to a statement. Schools must be wary of labelling parents as over-anxious or 'pushy' as by doing so they may tend to disregard the concern. Parents want the best for their children and, therefore, it would be helpful if their worries were either talked through or they were given generalised information such as the following:

*Explanation of specific learning difficulties and other learning problems*

- Some children find the process of reading and spelling very difficult. They may have no problems with other subjects and seem to be better at answering than coping with the written word. If these children have specific learning difficulties then they learn to read and spell in different ways from the other children in their class.

- Some children have learning difficulties because they have missed a lot of schooling. Some may have had health problems or sensory problems such as 'glue ear' which have hindered their rate of learning. Some children may have changed schools a lot and may have been taught by different methods. Some children are generally slower and will learn everything at a slower pace.

- There are no 'cures' as such for children with specific learning difficulties. However, given appropriate teaching the difficulties may lessen. Often reading improves but spelling may remain a long-term problem.

- Not all children with specific learning difficulties have the same problems. Some have mild problems and can be helped within the ordinary classroom. Some have more serious and long-term problems so may have to be assessed by an advisory teacher and/or educational psychologist. These children may be given special teaching programmes.

*Identification of a child with specific learning difficulties*
Specific learning difficulties may be detected if the child:

- fails to make the expected progress in reading and spelling even though there seems to be no reason for this;

- shows uneven performance in school subjects especially where progress is seen in those subjects and those areas which do not require spelling and reading performance;

- is taking a long time to develop the skills of learning to read and to write;

- shows there are problems with visual memory so that it is hard to remember words by sight for both reading and spelling;

- shows there are problems with auditory memory so that it is hard to use sounds for reading and spelling. There are also problems with saying rhymes and giving rhyming words;

- shows there are organisational and general memory problems so that the child finds it difficult to remember things like messages.

*What the school might undertake if a child has specific learning difficulties*

- If specific learning difficulties is suspected then the school will try different types of teaching.

- There are school-based stages which can be put into operation.

- There are particular programmes of work which can be put into operation in order to help the child.

- The 'special arrangements' procedures for tests and examinations can be requested and put into practice.

*What the LEA might undertake if the child's specific learning difficulties are deemed severe*

- The roles of any LEA 'specialist' should be explained.

- The criteria for making a request for statutory assessment and the LEA procedures for dealing with this should be gone through.

- The benefits of a statement should be identified.

*Parental assistance for a child with specific learning difficulties*

- Sometimes specific learning difficulties run in families so there may be someone else with a similar problem.

- Families can help a child who has specific learning difficulties by:
  - being patient when the child has problems remembering
  - being supportive and helpful in trying to help the child organise his or her day
  - making sure that other members of the family do not laugh at the child's mistakes or label him or her 'thick' or 'stupid'. If the child loses confidence, learning becomes more difficult.

- Families can help to teach the child with specific learning difficulties but it depends on the particular child and the family. Some children find it hard to see their parents as teachers. Some parents find it hard to take on the teacher role, especially because they have to keep very patient and encouraging. Very close liaison should take place with the school and the teachers. Parents should try to undertake things as the school would do, so good home–school information is needed.

Pointers like this can be talked through with both the parents and the teacher making factual statements about the child which fit with any particular detail that is raised. Parents should be able to add other observations and the teacher can show evidence of the child's performance from classwork and National Curriculum attainments. If it is felt that the child should be placed on either Stage 1 or 2 then this should happen with a built-in review date so that the parent knows when the next meeting will be.

In order to help children with specific learning difficulties to consolidate their learning in school it is important that they work with their parents at home. There will be some families who will not be able to cope here and these families should not be penalised by the school. Parents will have to be given direct instructions as to what to do with particular programmes, but in general the following suggestions for parents can be given:

- Be positive.

- Be patient.

- Praise and encourage.

- Try to avoid failure and stress situations.

- Listen to the child's problems and try to understand them.

- Keep a sense of humour.

- Know when to change the activity.

- Do not compete with a favourite television programme or other activity.

- Work with the child individually if other siblings distract or are more able.

- Share your observations with the school.

- Help with organisational problems.

- Help with but do not 'do' homework.

- Encourage regular practice in problem areas.

It would be more helpful for all concerned if parents could learn to recognise and accept their child as being 'learning different' rather than having a 'deficit' in his or her learning. A specific learning difficulty, unlike an illness, cannot be readily 'cured'. But it can be helped by teaching to the child's strengths and alongside this working to overcome the weaknesses. Strategies can be given to enable the child to access the curriculum areas and to help any of his or her particular organisational problems. Positive support rather than expressions of concern will foster strong and clear feelings of self-worth in the child. If children are to cope with difficulties, wherever they are on the continuum of specific learning difficulties, they will need both encouragement and acceptance, especially from their immediate families.

# Conclusion

The ultimate aim for parents, teachers, school and the LEA is that the support given to and the programme provided for any particular child with specific learning difficulties will show success. Correct assessment and correct ways of meeting needs can show progress. Each pupil has to be assessed on an individual basis and his or her needs met in the best way possible, whether this is within the school, with the additional help of a statement or in rarer cases in other types of school. No single solution meets every case.

*An example to show the progress that may be made since first identification was made*

Concern was felt about Joe's literacy problems when he was 5 years 8 months and he was referred to the advisory teacher for learning support at 6 years 6 months who found the following:

- He lacked confidence and although articulate was very quiet in class.

- His receptive language abilities were very high.

- His poor short-term visual memory meant that he could recall six keywords and a few other words from the reading scheme books. He would only write four words independently.

- He had visual directional and sequencing problems.

- He had poor phonological problems (unable to rhyme and cope with whispered blendings) although he could hear initial sounds and write some.

- His handwriting was very poor.

- He had organisational problems.

Programmes of work were suggested and carried out. At 8 years 2 months he was seen by an LEA educational psychologist and his IQ was measured as above average. At 9 years 3 months he was given a statement of special educational needs and two hours' teaching was set up as well as the in-school support.

At 10 years 7 months the advisory teacher for specific learning difficulties reviewed his progress and found:

- He was very confident and pleased about his progress and he took part in all classroom activities.

- He sight-read with ease 196/200 keywords.

- His NRA A reading accuracy midpoint was 7.6 years and he used context and phonic decoding skills.

- He had worked through a phonic programme up to vowel digraphs.

- His spelling age measured at 7.2 years on Schonell Spelling Test and his attempts at unknown words showed that he could use quite reasonable sound letter patterns. He could write a great deal of work which would communicate with the reader.

His continued problems were self-organisation and directional problems. The programme would continue into the secondary sector until his reading became at least at a functional level where he was felt to be able to access the separate subject areas.

All children have individual needs of some kind. Children with specific learning difficulties have very particular individual needs. Specific learning difficulties should not be considered a 'handicapping condition' but rather as something which should be recognised as distinct to the individual which requires description and attention. These children are 'learning different'. The majority of children with specific learning difficulties can be helped within school without the support of a statement of special educational needs.

The first important factor is the individual's self-esteem – his or her acceptance and understanding of the problem and his or her ability to be positive when the 'going seems tough'. The second important factor is the understanding of others, of peers, family and teachers, so that everyone works with the individual to help him or her to either overcome the specific problems or to find strategies of working round them.

Owen, a 13-year-old boy of average intelligence with no measurable reading and spelling skills, declared 'it's the same principle' (meaning that the label he had been given of specific learning difficulties meant the same thing as unintelligence). Because of this perspective, he gave up on learning. A counterpart with similar intelligence and attainment levels, Michael, accessed his way into the mainstream curriculum with the words 'I'll have to do it my way.'

Teachers who care will want to help change any such negative views shown by pupils. And they will.

# Appendices

# Appendix 1
# A Basic Information Check-Sheet for Secondary Schools

The following can form a basic information sheet which can be given as it stands to secondary school members of staff. It will serve to give them some global factors about the problems experienced by pupils with specific learning difficulties and to give some hints about how to deal with such problems. However, lists such as these can be personalised, so two examples are also given.

SPOTLIGHT ON SPECIAL EDUCATIONAL NEEDS:
SPECIFIC LEARNING DIFFICULTIES

# INFORMATION FOR SUBJECT TEACHERS

*If you teach a pupil with specific learning difficulties he or she may:*

- have problems with the mechanical side to reading although understanding the content;

- be well able to cope orally;

- have problems with spelling. This can show in these respects:
  1. only simple words are written to avoid errors
  2. words are readable but incorrect
  3. words are unreadable;

- have poor numeracy skills;

- have problems with handwriting. Often poor handwriting is adopted to mask spelling errors;

- have problems with written work because of poor study skills;

- have problems with taking notes from dictation or copying notes from the board;

- have problems with following instructions;

- produce limited written work and homework;

- have low self-esteem and lack of confidence;

- be a slow worker because of difficulties;

- lack concentration;

- have organisational problems;

- become tired because of the concentration needed and, therefore, become inconsistent in performance.

*It would be helpful if you would:*
GENERALLY

- Praise and encourage and find something he or she is good at.

- Let him or her sit where you can help without doing so obtrusively.

- Encourage oral responses.

- Not always expect as much classwork or homework as from others.

- Try and vary the activities and break up sustained activities into smaller ones (small tasks).

- Use appropriate language both when talking and presenting written work.

- Use the computer if appropriate.

- Make work achievable.

- Examine your methods of assessment and maybe modify these.

- Involve parents and keep them informed of progress and problems.

- Use parents' help where appropriate.

- Use the blackboard as little as possible.

## WHERE READING IS CONCERNED

- Do not insist on reading out aloud if he or she finds this a problem.

- Help with unfamiliar subject words.

- Liaise with the special needs department or learning support advisory staff to help teach unfamiliar words or go through work to be read.

- Help with study skills (eg skimming/scanning/main points etc).

- Keep your own handwriting legible to facilitate pupils' reading.

## WHERE SPELLING IS CONCERNED

- Mark written work on content not spelling to encourage use of a wide vocabulary.

- Only correct a few errors.

- Teach necessary subject words – but do not overload.

- Liaise with the special needs department or learning support advisory staff to help teach necessary words.

- Allow him or her to read back the work if words are unreadable.

- Do not expect dictionary work as this may be too difficult to be used.

## WHERE WRITTEN WORK IS CONCERNED

- Encourage him or her to smarten up handwriting but do not expect it to be changed.

- Do not ask him or her to write out work again unless he or she has not taken any care.

- Either give more time or allow another pupil to make a carbon copy if note-taking is difficult.

- Give less written work.

© Dorothy Smith, 1996
NASEN Enterprises Ltd.

*A personalised information sheet for a pupil transferring to the
secondary sector at Stage 2*

## INFORMATION FOR SUBJECT TEACHERS

GERMAINE _____ d.o.b. _____

_____HIGH

   Germaine has some specific learning difficulties which have affected
his reading and spelling skills. He is on a Record of Support Stage 2. He
also suffers from light sensitivity (Scotopic Sensitivity Syndrome) and
uses overlays to read through. Germaine can read texts around the 10
years readability level but his understanding is better than his oral reading.
He should be able to cope with most of the texts given in the subject
areas. He finds small, closely packed print a problem. His written work
communicates rather than containing totally accurate spellings.
Germaine may find it difficult to copy notes from the board.

*It would be helpful if you would:*
GENERALLY

 • Be aware of his SSS problems and that he is unable to use his
   overlays for any work other than reading texts.

WHERE READING IS CONCERNED

 • Do not insist on oral reading if he finds this a problem.

 • Help with unfamiliar subject words.

 • Help with study skills (eg skimming/scanning/main points etc).

 • Keep your own handwriting legible to facilitate his reading.

WHERE SPELLING IS CONCERNED

 • Mark written work on content not spelling to encourage use of a wide
   vocabulary.

- Only correct a few errors.

- Teach necessary subject words – but do not overload.

- Liaise with the special needs department or learning support advisory staff to help teach necessary words.

## WHERE WRITTEN WORK IS CONCERNED

- Either give more time or allow another pupil to make a carbon copy if note-taking is difficult.

---

*A personalised information sheet for a pupil transferring to the secondary sector with a statement of special educational needs*

### INFORMATION FOR SUBJECT TEACHERS

ALEX _____ d.o.b. _____
_____HIGH

Alex has specific learning difficulties which mean that his reading and spelling attainments do not match his general abilities. He is an intelligent pupil. He has a statement of special educational needs. Alex can read texts around the 7 year readability level. His written work is weak and there may be times when his spellings do not communicate. Alex will find it difficult to take notes from dictation or copy notes from the board and he may have difficulties with following instructions. It is possible that he will produce less written work and homework than his peers. Alex has quite good self-esteem but this took a long time to build up so it is felt that his present self-confidence is fragile. He has some speech and articulation problems.

*It would be helpful if you would:*
GENERALLY

- Praise and encourage and find something he is good at.

- Let him sit where you can help without doing so obtrusively.

- Encourage oral responses.

- Not always expect as much classwork or homework as from others.

- Use appropriate language both when talking and presenting written work.

- Make work achievable.

- Examine your methods of assessment and maybe modify these.

- Use the blackboard as little as possible.

## WHERE READING IS CONCERNED

- Do not insist on oral reading as he will find this a problem.

- Help with unfamiliar subject words.

- Liaise with the special needs department or learning support advisory staff to help teach unfamiliar words or go through work to be read.

- Keep your own handwriting legible to facilitate his reading.

## WHERE SPELLING IS CONCERNED

- Mark written work on content not spelling to encourage use of a wide vocabulary.

- Only correct a few errors.

- Teach necessary subject words – but do not overload.

- Liaise with the special needs department or learning support advisory staff to help teach necessary words.

- Allow him to read back the work if words are unreadable.

- Do not expect dictionary work as this may be too difficult to be used.

WHERE WRITTEN WORK IS CONCERNED

- Encourage him to smarten up handwriting but do not expect it to be changed.

- Do not ask him to write out work again unless he has not taken any care.

- Either give more time or allow another pupil to make a carbon copy if note-taking is difficult.

- Give less written work.

- Allow alternatives for recording if it is felt that he cannot get his thoughts down on paper.

# Appendix 2
# Some Definitions of Other Specific Learning Difficulties

## Dyslexia

Dr Chris Singleton gives two definitions when lecturing on the subject. In simple terms he states it is 'an unexpected difficulty in acquiring effective literacy skills'. Early definitions of dyslexia were concerned solely with reading attainment and only in more recent years has dyslexia broadened to take in other areas of learning. However, because this rather uncomplicated statement does not seem to give the full picture, Dr Singleton has amplified it. The definition then states that 'developmental dyslexia is a constitutional condition which results in differences in some aspects of information processing by the brain and which causes difficulties in specific areas of learning, particularly literacy skills'. He specifies that it is helpful to think of differences rather than deficits, for a difference in the way an individual learns should lead to a difference in the way he or she is taught.

## Dyspraxia

Dyspraxia is also a probable constitutional condition where the dyspraxic individual has problems with learning and acquiring patterns of movement. It is a dysfunction of co-ordination and shows itself in poor spatial awareness, and problems with handwriting and gross and fine motor control. For some children there are problems with the muscles which co-ordinate the movement needed for speech. Therefore, some children have verbal and/or articulatory dyspraxia where they find it difficult to speak clearly and to express themselves efficiently. Speech therapists and occupational therapists may become involved with children whose dyspraxia is quite severe.

## Dysgraphia

Because of the problems that some individuals were found to have with graphomotor (handwriting) skills and other fine motor skills (such as using scissors, tying laces), the term 'dysgraphia' was employed as another sub-set of the specific learning difficulties family. However, 'dyspraxia' seems to be the term more commonly used today showing that terminology can alter over the years.

## Dysphasia

This is a specific problem of language rather than of articulation problems. Language difficulties can either be receptive or expressive or a mixture of both. Receptive language is concerned with the understanding of words and how they are used. Expressive language is concerned with how one uses words to convey meaning. A specialised speech and language assessment is usually needed in order to gain the knowledge necessary for identification and remediation of severe language problems. However, there are certain language behaviours that can alert teachers and parents to a particular problem especially if these persist past the age when they are acceptable.

## Dyscalculia

This term means that an individual has a particular specific problem in the area of numeracy. Some children seem to have solely this one 'block' within their learning capabilities. Many others who have specific learning difficulties in acquiring literacy skills also have similar problems with number. Problems with short and long-term memories, directional confusion, sequencing and perceptual difficulties, and problems with spatial awareness can make learning number sequences, tables, place value and so forth extremely difficult. Added to these can come the more generalised problems pertaining to mathematics such as the language of mathematics and mathematical problem solving. It is felt by many that there is less of a stigma in being termed 'innumerate' rather than being termed 'illiterate' and that individuals can cope in life with poorly developed numeracy skills.

# Appendix 3
# Other 'Companions' to the Specific Learning Difficulties Range

## Scotopic Sensitivity Syndrome (SSS) or Irlen Syndrome

This can be termed a condition which is often found alongside other learning difficulties rather than a learning difficulty in itself. Its origin is from America where Helen Irlen first discovered that certain individuals found it easier to read through coloured overlays. SSS is a perceptual dysfunction not a problem of actual eyesight and screeners always recommend that a thorough eyesight examination is undertaken if SSS problems are suspected and later detected. For some individuals it seems that the brain has difficulties with processing information from full spectral light. It is not a condition just experienced by those with specific learning difficulties but many pupils with specific literacy problems particularly in the visual field may also have SSS. Research continues to be carried out into the reasons why some individuals suffer from this syndrome.

There are a range of problems which can be experienced by individuals who are said to have SSS. These are:

- light sensitivity:
  where individuals find it a problem working under strong sunlight or fluorescent lighting;

- black-white contrast:
  where individuals find it difficult to cope with the black print on bright white pages;

- print distortion:
  where individuals find that letters on the page move or even disappear;

- span of recognition:
  where difficulties occur with keeping on track on the page when reading;

- concentration and attention:
  where individuals become very sleepy or restless when having to stay on task during reading and writing activities;

- distance and spatial relationship problems:
  where there are difficulties with judging differences in distance, height and depth.

Some opticians use an apparatus called an Intuitive Colorimeter to diagnose these problems and then to prescribe coloured overlays or tinted lenses (glasses). Also there are several Irlen Centres throughout Great Britain with trained practitioners who do likewise. The Irlen Centres train teachers and other adults as pre-screeners who, after asking a range of questions and carrying out a series of activities, can judge whether the pupil needs to use an overlay or a combination of overlays in order to read more efficiently.

After being given either overlays or the tinted glasses, many individuals show a marked difference in the way they cope with the reading process. However, it has to be noted that overlays and glasses do not 'cure' reading problems. They take away any strain or visual 'anomalies' that might have previously been experienced.

## ADD (Attention Deficit Disorder)

ADD is a form of brain dysfunction where there is chemical imbalance within the brain. This affects the child so that he or she finds it extremely difficult to concentrate and maintain attention. There is impulsivity of behaviour which leads the child to say or act without thinking first. The child also becomes hyperactive and finds it hard to listen to those in authority and act on what is said. Behaviour modification programmes are organised but also medication is prescribed. These help to control the behaviour so that the child is more able to learn.

It is often queried what is the difference between a child with behavioural problems and one with ADD. In brief, one should look at where the unacceptable behaviours occur. If they are widespread within lessons and situations that are enjoyable and also within the home situation, they are probably those pertaining to ADD and are not of the child's volition. If they occur only in certain lessons, such as the difficult ones of literacy and/or numeracy, then behaviour management plus some change within the learning-teaching situation should change the undesirable situation.

In some educational circles ADD (and its companion ADHD, Attention Deficit Hyperactivity Disorder) is part of the dyslexia 'stable'. Others recognise that any child might suffer from ADD.

# Appendix 4
# Information About the Language Areas

**Receptive (understanding) language**
The child may have problems with:

- following instructions and needs constant repetition;

- understanding jokes, language that is not literal (tends to be a literalist);

- understanding vocabulary;

- comprehension on reading assessments which score at a weaker level than the scores on the accuracy reading level;

- listening skills which will be weak;

- poor understanding of time vocabulary;

- understanding and giving rhymes;

- phonological awareness (cannot understand the segmentation of words into syllables and/or phonemes).

**Expressive (using) language**
The child may have problems with:

- recalling words (uses descriptions etc and use of time and position words);

- the use and misuse of pronouns, past tenses, plurals;

- articulation (plus the production of malapropisms);

- labelling;

- descriptive and imaginative language which is simply and poorly expressed;

- phonological awareness (cannot segment words into syllables and/or phonemes);

- sentence construction (either speaks with long confused sentences or only uses short phrases or one word answers);

- retelling events, stories or expanding what has been said.

# Appendix 5
# Simultaneous Oral Spelling Techniques (SOS)

This method of learning to spell is particularly useful for those children who have poor visual retentive memories and who need to learn commonly used words (irregular high-frequency or keywords).

Before embarking on this method, the teacher should make sure that the child is able to recognise and say all the names of the letters of the alphabet, both upper and lower case. It is also more beneficial if the child has learnt to write in a cursive script so that the hand flows through the letters.

*Method*

- The adult writes the word and says it.

- The child looks at it and repeats the word.

- The child spells the word out loud saying the letter names.

- The child copies the word (in a cursive script if possible), naming the letters as they are written.

- The child reads the written word.

- The child writes over the word saying the letter names.

- The child covers the word and writes it from memory, continuing to say the letters in their correct sequence.

- The child checks the written attempt with the original.

As well as writing and saying the word, an extra step can be added where plastic or wooden letters are used to sequence the letters correctly before the child attempts the written version.

# References and Further Reading

Alston, J (1995) *Assessing and Promoting Writing Skills – New Edition.* NASEN: Tamworth.

Arnold, H (1983) *Listening to Children Reading.* Hodder and Stoughton: London.

Augur, J (undated) *Dyslexia – Early Help – Better Future.* The British Dyslexia Association: Reading.

Beveridge, S (1996) *Learning Difficulties.* NASEN: Tamworth.

Bill, G (1995) *Governor's Guide to Special Educational Needs in Mainstream School.* NASEN: Tamworth.

Bradley, L (1984) *Assessing Reading Difficulties.* NFER-Nelson: Windsor.

Clay, M (1985) *The Early Detection of Reading Difficulties – Third Edition.* Heinemann: Auckland.

Connor, M (1994) 'Specific learning difficulty (dyslexia) and interventions'. *Support for Learning,* 9, 3, pp.114–119.

Cripps, C and Peters, M (1983) *Catchwords.* Harcourt Brace Jovanovich: London.

Crisfield, J and Smythe I (1993) *The Dyslexia Handbook 1993/4.* The British Dyslexia Association: Reading.

Crisfield, J (1994) *The Dyslexia Handbook 1995.* The British Dyslexia Association: Reading.

Crisfield, J (1996) *The Dyslexia Handbook 1996.* The British Dyslexia Association: Reading.

Crombie, M (1991) *Specific Learning Difficulties (Dyslexia) – A Teacher's Guide.* Jordanhill Sales and Publications: Glasgow (out of print).

DfEE (1994) *The Code of Practice on the Identification and Assessment of Special Educational Needs.* HMSO: London.

The Dyspraxia Trust (undated), *Praxis Makes Perfect*. The Dyspraxis Trust: Buckinghamshire.

*Dyslexia – Your Questions Answered* (undated). The British Dyslexia Association: Reading.

El Naggar, O (1996) *Specific Learning Difficulties in Mathematics: A Classroom Approach*. NASEN: Tamworth.

Gordon, M and Smith H (1995) *A Secondary School Approach*. NASEN: Tamworth.

Helier, Cyril (1994) 'Closing the gap: Compensating for literacy delay in children with specific learning difficulties/dyslexia'. *Support for Learning*, 9, 4, pp.162–165.

Irlen, H (1991) *Reading by the Colours*. Avery Publishing Group: New York.

Luton, K (1995) *Policy Development for Special Educational Needs: A Primary Approach*. NASEN: Tamworth.

Malone, G and Smith, D (1996) *Learning to Learn: Developing study skills with children who have special educational needs*. NASEN: Tamworth.

Peters, M and Smith, B (1993) *Spelling in Context*. NFER-Nelson: Windsor.

Pinsent, P (ed.) (1990) *Children with Literacy Difficulties*. Fulton: London.

Pollock, J and Walker, E (1994) *Day-to-Day Dyslexia in the Classroom*. Routledge: London.

Pumfrey, P and Reason, R (1991) *Specific Learning Difficulties (Dyslexia) – Challenges and Responses*. NFER-Nelson: Windsor.

Reason, R and Boote, R (1994) *Learning Difficulties in Reading and Writing*. Routledge: London.

Smith, D, Shirley, J and Visser, J (1996) *Teachers and Parents: Together for Reading*. NASEN: Tamworth.

Snowling, M (ed.) (1996) *Dyslexia, Speech and Language: A Practitioner's Handbook*. Whurr Publishers: London.

Tansley, P and Panckhurst, J (1981) *Children with Specific Learning Difficulties*. NFER-Nelson: Windsor.

Tyre, C (1994) *Specific Learning Difficulties*. QEd Publications: Lichfield.

Warin, S (1996) *Implementing the Code of Practice: Individual Education Plans*. NASEN: Tamworth.

Warnock Report (1978) *Special Educational Needs*. HMSO: London.

# Materials and Tests

Brand, V, *Spelling Made Easy*. Egon Publishers Ltd: Baldock.

*Crown Reading Programme* (1980) Nelson.

Distar, McGraw-Hill-SRA.

Dunn et al., *British Picture Vocabulary Scale*. NFER-Nelson: Windsor.

Elliott, L, *S.T.R.A.N.D.S.,* Winchester SO23 8UG.

Franklin Elementary Spellmaster (and other products), Electronic Learning Products, Reading.

*Fuzzbuzz Reading Scheme*. Oxford University Press: Oxford.

*Graded Word Reading Test*. NFER-Nelson: Windsor.

Hickey, K (1992) *The Hickey Multisensory Language Course: 2nd edition*. Whurr Publishers: London.

Hornsby, B and Shear, F (1974) *Alpha to Omega*. Heinemann: London.

McNally, J and Murray, M (1985) *Key Words to Literacy*. School Master Publishing Company.

Moseley, D and Nicol, C (1989) *ACE Dictionar.* LDA: Cambridge.

Neale, M, *Analysis of Reading Ability.* NFER-Nelson: Windsor.

North, C and Parker, M (1993), *Phonological Awareness Pack.* Summerhill, Althorne CM3 6BY.

Raven, J, *Progressive Matrices and Vocabulary Scales.* NFER-Nelson: Windsor.

Richards, J (1988) *Attack Your Reading, Writing, Spelling Problems – Our Way.*

Salford Sentence Reading Test. Hodder and Stoughton: London.

Singleton, C (1996) *KEYSTAGE 1 CoPS.* Chameleon Educational Systems Ltd.

Stone et al., *Beat Dyslexia.* LDA: Wisbech.

*THRASS,* Collins Educational.

Vincent, D and de la Mare, M, *Individual Reading Analysis.* NFER-Nelson: Windsor.

Vincent, D and de la Mare, M, *New Reading Analysis.* NFER-Nelson: Windsor.

Wellington Square, Nelson.

Wendon, L (1987) *Letterland Teaching Programmes 1 and 2.* Letterland Ltd: Cambridge.

Young, D (1983) *Parallel Spelling Tests.* Hodder and Stoughton: London.

## Helpful Addresses

The British Dyslexia Association, 98 London Road, Reading RG1 5AU.
RSA
The Dyslexia Institute, 133 Gresham Road, Staines, Middlesex TW18 2AJ.
Helen Arkell Dyslexia Centre, Frensham, Farnham, Surrey GU10 3BW.
Irlen Centres (see local telephone directories for the nearest regional centre).
Taskmaster Resources, Taskmaster Ltd, Morris Road, Leicester LE2 6BR.